Lessons Learned

To my dear friends ...

Aaron, Lori, Benjamin, and Luke

I love you guys!

Randy

11 - 7 - 2012

Lessons Learned

Practical Insights into Developing an Effective
Adult or Student Choir Ministry

Randy Edwards

MorningStar
MUSIC PUBLISHERS

MorningStar Music Publishers, Inc.
1727 Larkin Williams Road, St. Louis, MO 63026-2024
www.morningstarmusic.com

Library of Congress Cataloging-in-Publication Data

Edwards, Randy, 1954-
  Lessons learned : practical insights into developing an effective adult or student choir ministry / Randy Edwards.
      p. cm.
  Includes bibliographical references and index.
  ISBN 978-0-944529-56-0 (alk. paper)
  1. Choirs (Music) 2. Ministers of music--Vocational guidance. 3. Church work with youth. I. Title.
  MT88.E28 2012
  782.5'3023--dc23
                        2012031780

Cover and book design: Kristen Schade

To

BABS BAUGH, JACKIE MOORE, AND JULIE CLOUD
members of the Eula Mae and John Baugh Foundation

for their friendship, support, partnership, and generosity to YouthCUE,
allowing me to give time and energy to my passion of student choir ministry,
and extending the love of their late parents and grandparents

EULA MAE and JOHN BAUGH
Christians, Baptists, Humanitarians, Philanthropists

Table of Contents

Acknowledgments

I have been thinking about writing this book for a good while—a few years, actually. Having randomly sketched outlines, phrases, concepts, and illustrations, I have sporadically captured thoughts on a dedicated legal pad, a Word file named "New Book," and just in my memory.

A few months ago, the season seemed ripe for the commencement of this project. I began writing in earnest a couple of months prior to the busiest time of the year for YouthCUE programming—spring and summer. There has been a window of a few weeks to get the book together and to the publisher, thus I have had a great deal of help getting the manuscript submitted by the deadline.

YouthCUE has become a passion for a number of people over the years, including the wonderful staff at our home office: Preston Edwards, Tina McCartney, Lois Gagné, Daniel Zamora, Jill Clay, and a heavenly host of volunteers. My manuscript assistants, Susan Spoon, Truett Edwards, and Gabriel Gagné have helped me stay on schedule and have provided perfect touches of timely insight and guidance. Without all of these, there would be no book.

I am so grateful to my children: Preston, Ashley, and Kathryn, who have always been so wonderfully supportive and affirming of their dad's efforts. They have provided me support, strength, and encouragement in ways they do not even realize, and it has been that way since the days they were born. Their contributions to the dream of student choirs have been immeasurable.

The support of my own community of faith, Woodland Baptist Church in San Antonio, has been utterly enormous. This church family exemplifies more than any church I have experienced what it means to be in happy fellowship with each other while in joyous communion with the Lord. Woodland is also a part of the YouthCUE dream in a myriad of affirming ways.

We extend great thanks and appreciation to Mark Lawson at MorningStar Music, who believes in youth choirs and is highly supportive of our efforts in numerous ways. Through the YouthCUE Anthem Series and incalculable support behind the scenes, Mark and his staff are not only wonderful colleagues but also great friends.

Finally and perhaps most importantly, we are so grateful to the women and men in the YouthCUE network who work long and diligently at their ministries with students. Far outside the spotlights, thousands of directors are, as we speak, working faithfully to bring beauty, passion, scripture, compassion, and ministry into the lives of teenagers all over the world. We salute all of them, and we are honored to be connected in some small way with them and their ministries. They are our heroes.

Introduction

Through twenty-one years of ministry within the YouthCUE network, it has been my pure privilege, joy, and honor to be connected and networked with thousands of youth choir directors and hundreds of thousands of students. We have worked hard together, studied, learned, been inspired, and hopefully become much more informed about this phenomenon called youth choir.

I mentioned this in the introduction to the first book, published in 2000, and I'll say it again after putting together a second effort: this is not a comprehensive text on how to build a ministry with youth choir. It is our hope that it will be provocative, but it could never be complete or comprehensive. For one thing, culture is changing too rapidly for that to ever happen. Secondly, there would never be enough time to write such a work, and if someone did, it would be so thick that no one could afford it or have any interest in reading it!

Throughout the book, we use "youth choir" and "student choir" interchangeably. Most student choirs are currently comprised of grades 6–12, but there are plenty of exceptions to that rule. It is my hope that what follows will be helpful and inspirational to you, regardless of the breakdown of your choir. It is also my hope and prayer that this book might inspire some directors to begin a student choir in their church or community, perhaps for the first time. If you do that, I and all the resources of YouthCUE would be privileged to be your partner every step of the way!

God bless us all as we reach out in the name of Christ to those students who need to experience all the beauty, passion, and joy the Savior has to offer. May music and our developing youth choirs be but one way of celebrating this glorious, abundant life!

Happy Singing!

Lesson One
Beauty

God's beautiful world, God's beautiful world,
I love God's beautiful world.
He made it for you. He made it for me.
I love God's beautiful world.
—Aurora M. Shumate

I was first exposed to this little song when I was three or four and, to this day, I can still sing it flawlessly. I think it must go with me wherever I go, with its lilting 6/8 melody pulsating throughout my head and heart without my even realizing it. Sometimes, I think its tempo is literally setting the speed of my stride. It seems to seep from the pores of my skin when I stand in awesome wonder of a mountain range or in total amazement of yet another utterly unique sunrise. The melody manifests itself on a crowded freeway as often as in a silent national park. It surfaces as regularly on the poverty-ridden streets of the south side of San Antonio as in the gated communities on the prestigious Santa Barbara coastline.

My Sunday School teachers in early life—my mother, Mrs. Sanders, Mrs. Banning, Mrs. Little, and Mrs. Moody—somehow conveyed the importance of identifying beauty and finding some way of celebrating it. They themselves noticed it, and they showed me how to discover it for myself. They allowed me space and freedom to wallow in the wonder of it all. They taught me how to sing about it and recognize the dynamic hand of God at its center.

In nature. Through colors, shades, and hues. Through art and the nuances of shape, shadow, and asymmetry. In creatures great and small. In rocks and trees and skies and seas. Through motion. And in music. As my teachers recognized it, pointed it out, and celebrated it with glee, I caught the fever and passion from them. I, like many students, was able to take it and run with it beyond what my teachers were able to do. Fifty years later, I love it when my students do the same.

The celebration of beauty was not just something my early teachers dreamed up. Beauty was invented by God, and the teachers were just inviting me to take a headlong plunge into the living stream of divine abundance.

The perception of beauty is a moral test.
—Henry David Thoreau

Like many other lessons in life, I'm not sure that the appreciation of beauty is something which can be adequately taught. How can one guarantee a lesson learned just because it has been well transmitted? We cannot assure it, because something has to happen internally if the student is to fall in love with beauty. The student himself has the final word.

But even though the love of beauty cannot be fully taught as such, it can certainly be caught and learned, and developed. Like an infectious disease, one teacher of beauty can most certainly spread the gem of a germ to dozens, hundreds, and even thousands of open-minded students close at hand. That number can and does escalate into the millions employing the current wonders of technology. Ask Eric Whitacre about that. Not only *can* it be done, but it *is* being done every day in huge cities, small towns, and rural communities across the world.

It is not sufficient to see and to know the beauty of a work.
We must feel and be affected by it.
—Voltaire

As directors of student choirs, it is our responsibility—yes, our unspeakable joy—to introduce teenagers to new forms of beauty. Teaching them to spot beauty is a huge part of the "teaching them to observe all things that I have commanded you" part of the Great Commission. Alas, many of the students who gather under our tutelage may not have been taught "God's Beautiful World" as children. They can neither sing it with their voices, hear it with their ears, nor feel it in their hearts. Their stomachs are empty of that basic sustaining nourishment … spiritual comfort food. It will be up to us to introduce the concept, nurture its reality, and encourage its fruit to grow.

We musicians have music as our primary tool—but not only music. There is also nature, art, science, dance, craftsmanship, athleticism, activism, friendship, compassion, philanthropy (in the broadest sense of the word), mission endeavors, and acts of kindness which are never really random. All these arenas and more hold displays of beauty for observant eyes of all ages.

Nature is God's first missionary. Where there is no Bible there are sparkling stars.
Where there are no preachers there are spring times ...
If a person has nothing but nature,
then nature is enough to reveal something about God.
—Max Lucado

A caveat must be cited here. It may seem obvious, but it still needs to be said outright: not everything in this world is beautiful. Humankind has done a pretty effective job of completely destroying beauty in some locations, stifling its growth in too many instances, and pouring the poison of social dysfunction over it in others. Everything is not beautiful in its own way. However, many masks of exterior ugliness contain hidden beauties that can be uncovered and restored by a divine healing relationship, a touch that can be provided us by loving teachers and ministers.

Never lose an opportunity of seeing anything beautiful,
for beauty is God's handwriting.
—Ralph Waldo Emerson

If we can teach teenagers to recognize, respect, and celebrate God's beauty, the gift we give them will be eternal in richness and everlasting through time. The gift, when accepted and personally experienced, will be neither forgotten nor minimized.

Unfortunately and even sadly, most of us student choir leaders have far more love and passion inside us than we have heretofore been willing to express. For reasons unknown, we tend to keep controlling lids on our enthusiasm and effervescence for the beauties around us, allowing only small bits and pieces of joy to flow forth into our rehearsals and ministerial relationships. Based upon YouthCUE's observation over the past two decades, the holding back—this reluctance to express the depth of our artistic impulses to our students—is a huge impediment to the choir development as a whole. In many cases, the director has become so emotionally walled in that he or she is unable to provide the strong leadership needed and desperately desired. When this happens (and it almost always occurs very gradually), the damage inflicted is far greater than the other excuses we directors may list for our choir's failure: church schedules, no support from parents, lack of commitment from the students, peer staff reticence.

There are ditches on both sides of the road. Yes, it is possible to become so free-wheeling and spontaneous that we become out of control, loose cannons. When we take our glee entirely too far, or when we go to seed on our own creative impulses, our students will think of us as "just plain weird." But the higher danger for most of us is on the other end of the continuum. The vast majority of us will become so predictable, so static, so controlled and flat-lined that our choirs will simply suffer from a lack of fresh oxygen.

If the full extent of our music consists only of singing the right notes to the correct texts at the appropriate tempi, we are missing an enormous component that music (in its best forms, exquisite manifestations of beauty) has to offer today's students. If we as conductors never get goose bumps—or if we do but never tell the students about them—we are shortchanging their experience and holding their spirits at bay from the life-giving stream of beauty. Can we do more than beat out a 4/4 pattern and give the correct cues? Will we dare to be expressive, passionate disciples and lavish lovers of beauty who will color our groups with hues, shades, and nuances too glorious for words?

If I did not believe we can be more effective in helping students discover beauty, I would not have attempted to write this book. I believe there is far more inside most of us than we are daring to express or let out.

The future belongs to those who believe
in the beauty of their dreams.
—Eleanor Roosevelt

When I take in a scene of true beauty, I find it very difficult to turn and walk away. It is even more difficult to walk away unaffected. How can anyone take a long, distant gaze at the Grand Canyon and not be mesmerized? How could any kid turn away from Niagara Falls and say, "So what?" Is it possible to hike the hills and grassy slopes around the Swiss Alps and respond with, "Ho hum," or to observe a spectacular sunset and say, "What's the big deal?"

Yes, these underwhelming responses are possible, but they are not natural. Through overstimulation and technological overkill, some of us have become utterly desensitized to beauty because entertainment and other artificialities have robbed us of our natural, God-given "Wow!"s.

There is something in greatness that calls out for more greatness. Something about beauty seeks a partnering response for additional beauty. When I observe greatness—it matters not in what arena this may happen to be—I then want to turn and produce more greatness in *my own* arena. When I experience beauty, I gain a desire to produce a beautiful product of my own. When I respond in this way, I know that I am joining forces (meager as mine are) with the Creator of Beauty, the Author of Greatness, the God we love, follow, and serve.

I'm asking God for one thing, only one thing:
To live with him in his house my whole life long.
I'll contemplate his beauty; I'll study at his feet.
—Psalm 27:4 (*The Message*)

Take It to the Next Level

For directors, reenergize yourself by:

1. Listing three beautiful things you can see sitting right where you are. It's possible that you may have to stretch your neck or your imagination a bit to find three items, but, more than likely, you may find it difficult to stop with just three.

2. Identifying whether these named beauties are purely God-things (natural beauties) or if they also include a human touch or two.

3. Taking one beauty you have identified, right where you are, and seeking to give some type of expression to it. For instance, you might jot down some words to convey what you are feeling after having recognized this thing of beauty. Or you might hear an original tune going through your head and, if so, sing it out loud. If nothing original comes to mind, feel free to borrow an expression—a poem, a song, a description—from someone else. It's quite possible that a hymn, a scripture passage, or an anthem fragment has already begun running across your forehead like a news ticker in Times Square. Whatever it is, take the time and give the energy needed to express it. Don't run away from this task, because when we do, we are giving prophecy to what we will do in the presence of our students in rehearsals.

For directors interacting with students:

1. Ask your teens to identify something that helps them feel safe and loved.

2. Encourage your students to remember a time early in their lives when they realized that they, too, could give love.

3. Affirm their ability to see the hand of God at work in everyday life.

What you see above are not one-time tasks. In order to open the windows of beauty to millennial students, we must keep the processes before them regularly, even constantly. Some beauties are ever before us and others are in motion and fleeting.

> *Beauty is eternity gazing at itself in a mirror.*
> —Khalil Gibran

Lesson Two

Passion

Education is not the filling of a bucket, but the lighting of a fire.
—W. B. Yeats

Teaching is not a profession; it's a passion.
—Unknown

You and I could write several books just on the challenges we face as student choir directors. It may be ambitious to the point of pure arrogance to deal with both the challenges and some solutions in one little chapter, but here goes. Hubris or not, I would like to give it a try in hopes of finding some new clarity and focus on the subject of passion.

To be sure, the world has changed unimaginably over the past two decades, so much so that it is difficult to even list or measure the changes, much less fully assimilate them.

That being said, it seems most of us have done rather well at staying abreast of at least some of the sweeping technological changes. For instance, almost of all of us carry a cell phone of some kind, a virtual electronic wallet that allows us not only to field phone calls but also to check email, stay connected to Facebook, take, send, and receive text messages, photos and movies, check bank balances, and even to pay bills. And there's much, much more, since now "there's an app for that!"

Just using a cell phone on a daily (hourly, or perhaps minute-by-minute) basis continually reminds me that the world is a different place than it once was. It also reminds me that what is hot and cutting edge today could be obsolete in six months. RIP, my dear Blackberry. The development of the cell phone and all it can accomplish is emblematic of the many technological tricks available in every area of our lives. Now that we're well into a new millennium, even the *rate* of exponential advancement is going through the roof.

Using the latest technology to stay in touch with our students—this is an act of passion. At YouthCUE, we have taken note that hundreds of directors in our network are doing an admirable job of adapting to new technologies in relating to their teenagers. A few dozen directors are on the very cutting edge of what is available, and their ministries have been strengthened by this commitment to stay current. It is no small task, but a director need not necessarily be on the raw cutting edge of technology in order to have good, effective contact and communication with kids.

In a completely rational society, the best of us would aspire to be teachers and the rest of us would have to settle for something less, because passing civilization along from one generation to the next ought to be the highest honor and the highest responsibility anyone could have.
—Lee Iacocca

What follows may at first seem far afield from the thread of a director's passion for ministry. I encourage you to stay with me to discover where this discussion will land. However, what happens at the end of this chapter is not to be considered an ending. If properly understood, it is only a launching pad.

Actually, the hurdles, roadblocks, and detours we encounter ministering to this generation may not be as complex or impossible as we had once thought. More to the point, I believe we can outline seven uphill battles we face as we commit ourselves to minister to students through choral music. See if you agree.

1. *Entertainment*—Much of this involves technological entertainment, including video games, online games, social networking, etc … but the phenomenon is much broader than these. Professional and collegiate sporting events have risen to new elevations of sound, action, videography, showbiz, and marketing. The attraction will continue to increase with the development of even more bells and whistles. Blockbuster movie hits and concert venues continue to ratchet up levels of expectation. This is a generation entertained to the point of nearly losing good sense. In some ways, entertainment has become an addictive drug that dulls the senses and can provide a near total escape from reality.

2. *Instant gratification*—Waiting is universally viewed as utterly undesirable and dogmatically distasteful. We become horribly impatient waiting on slow computers or standing in line to make a purchase. We have probably all observed vehicles stuck in traffic whose gotta-keep-moving drivers will depart from the crowd to feverishly pursue alternate roads. Many times, these plan B routes will actually take longer to drive and will be three or four times the distance. However, they are appealing because the driver continues to move without having to wait. We are a society that would rather burn three times the fuel and take twice the time just to avoid the dreaded

stop-and-wait. Banks and credit card companies have made their billions on people who cannot take the wait.

3. *It's all about me*—Ironically, we regularly find the most selfish of attitudes being displayed by parents more than their offspring. Oftentimes, parents invoke the names of their children as they make their demands for special dispensations. "We have to meet the needs of our children" can usually be interpreted as, "You have to provide me what I want and now." In actuality, the demand may have little or nothing to do with the children and their perceived needs. Parents truly concerned about the wellbeing of their children will not continually demand that their children be handled with kid gloves. Instead, they would be concerned that their teens learn to survive and be prepared to thrive in an outside world that often cuts them little or no slack at all. Most teenagers themselves, even those from self-centered family units, intuitively desire more out of life than having the universe revolve around them. As student choir directors, we have the opportunity to offer them a healthy alternative. But beware that doing so will sometimes place us between papa and mama bear and the cubs. It can become a very tricky enterprise to support families without inadvertently coming between them.

4. *Traditional church has fallen on challenging times*—Here I am not primarily referring to traditional vs. contemporary worship styles, although this issue may be involved in some cases and to varying degrees. Regardless of a particular church's tradition—which may in fact include cutting edge contemporary music—the tradition is being challenged in this generation. Any church which has been around for a decade or more is in need of regular reevaluation of how it "does church" in the present and near future. The needed adjustments may be sweeping or slight, but recalibration is necessary just the same if the church is going to truly remain responsive and proactive in the millennial generation. Congregations bent on being lay-led are more often than not very slow on the uptake, sluggish and political in decision-making, overly meticulous in budget development and dwarfed in outreach and growth. CEO-led models are often too quick to jerk the congregation around, sometimes more committed to staying cutting edge than communicating the whole counsel of God, and are often fiscally wasteful. Somewhere in between lies a mystical balance, which wise, thoughtful church leadership will discover and dare to employ. Truly savvy congregations will be willing to keep their processes fluid and flexible in the future so the latest hierarchy does not become a dinosaur yet again. In this culture, organizational fossilization takes only a fraction of the time it did in the last millennium.

5. *Scheduling*—Churches big and small, urban, suburban, inner city, and rural are supremely challenged trying to carve out prime time for the extensive ministry buffets we feel obliged to offer our parishioners, particularly our children. Nothing burns more ministerial staff time and oil than this one challenging component.

6. *Lack of commitment to the long haul*—In an attempt to gain results now, churches often sacrifice in the long term what we know good and well to be crucially important. Does this bear a striking resemblance to *Number 2, Instant Gratification,* above? This is perhaps the most graphic example of how the pressures of secularism have invaded our sacred—which is supposed to mean "set apart"—houses of worship. Moreover, since it is our children and youth who are supposed to be the beneficiaries and torchbearers of long-term ministry, they and their futures are being sacrificed on the altars of frantic fixes, all in the name of the latest buzz word—"relevance."

7. *Over-commitment, compassion fatigue, and program burnout*—The first six hurdles converge and intersect to form our seventh challenge. The key word here is fatigue.

Let us now return to our second lesson, which deals with the indispensability of a passionate director. Any one of the seven hurdles above (or more, if you thought of others) might easily deter and fatally discourage any number of well-meaning student choir leaders. However, those of us who possess a holy passion for student choir ministry will figure out ways to turn the obvious hurdles into building materials.

Please do not misinterpret what I have just written to insinuate that it will be easy, simple, or quick.

The passionate journey is not for every musician, no more than a marathon is for every thirty-year-old. But those of us who have fire in our bones to see choral music stay vibrant and energized will take on the challenge. It will happen one small step at a time.

> *A teacher affects eternity;*
> *he can never tell where his influence stops.*
> —Henry Adams

For instance, relating to each of the seven hurdles listed above:

- With some concerted efforts and building of strong relationships with students over time, the desperate need for entertainment can be displaced in varying measures by the desire to accomplish personal excellence.

- By engaging a student in a serious study of scripture—anthem scripture texts very much count, particularly if they are explored, discussed, and applied—it is very possible to teach teenagers that there is value and virtue in waiting patiently for the right things.

- As we model compassion and caring on multiple levels, students can move beyond an attitude of "me first" into positive attitudes of servanthood, philanthropy, and self-sacrifice.

- Although their parents and grandparents may have assigned to churches labels and stereotypes, this generation of millennials could not care less about these exteriors. The values that matter the most are whether or not the church is consistent in its values and if it is effective in improving the communities and worlds around it.

- Once a student has discovered healthy socialization and personal spiritual value in a ministry or activity, she will normally figure out a way to fit it into her complex schedule. She may or may not have time to give to something of marginal worth, but with high value comes high commitment.

- Few adolescents will set out to invest themselves over a long term. Developmentally, most students are not yet capable of major future envisioning and will need to find definite value in their pursuits as they go. Through the relationships we develop with teenagers, we can affirm their positive priorities and encourage their good choices, pointing them to the reality that these will manifest significant fruit-bearing results in their futures. Notoriously short-sighted, adolescent students can be led to dream about their later lives and make strong choices in the present.

- One-on-one friendships with our students will open doors for occasions when they seek our input, advice, and counsel regarding their personal challenges. An astute director will recognize the signs of students in time binds and at particular stress points. The contribution we are able to make in these crucial moments will be highly valuable as the students grow and mature. Many will recall what we said and how we said it decades after the fact.

Those of us who do not possess this internal fire will find a plethora of other easier activities and opportunities to fill our lives; only genuinely passionate directors will be around for the whole process. These are the ones who will engage significantly with their students, becoming inspirations, friends, mentors, and unofficial guidance counselors. The rewards for passionate leadership are eternally enormous. You are invited to share the dream and do the work!

It's not that I'm so smart; it's just that I stay with problems longer.
—Albert Einstein

Take It to the Next Level

Directors, consider the following for yourselves:

1. On a scale of 1 to 10 (1 being the least, 10 being the most), subjectively rate your passion for working with students.

2. What do you think? Is this passion for student choir ministry something you can develop, or is it simply placed inside you by God?

3. How does your level of passion compare to your perception of the most successful student choir directors you have observed?

4. If you could push a magic button and provide your students anything you wish out of your cache of abilities, what would it be? Try to be as specific as possible in your description.

5. What is currently keeping you from pushing the magic button?

6. Can you ever see a time when and a place where you might be willing to move your student choir ministry out of the confines of the church and re-locate it in a larger, broader community?

For directors engaging with students, ask them the following:

1. What are you most passionate about? Why?

2. How many things do you think you can be truly passionate about? One? Four? Ten?

3. How do you know something is a passion for you?

4. Describe someone twenty years older than you who has dedicatedly fol-lowed his/her passion for many years. What are the characteristics you would like to emulate in this person?

Lesson Three
A Real Person

We do not exist for ourselves.
—Thomas Merton

Musicians are known to be a self-centered tribe. Actually, it makes a lot of sense that we would be. After all, if we find joy singing, playing, or performing in front of an audience, there must be a little show-off in there somewhere!

Furthermore, nine out of nine of us made it as professional musicians how? By working very hard and by the multiplied hours spent on *our* musical skills, practicing *our* scales, developing *our* tones, tuning *our* pitches, perfecting *our* techniques, memorizing *our* assigned repertoire, passing *our* exams and performing *our* final juries. In fact, so focused were we on *our* musical development that most of us employed private teachers to further focus on *our* musical and artistic advancements. Focusing on ourselves was not enough; in order to be at our best, we had to pay someone else to focus on us, too!

I'm reminded of Bette Midler's line in the movie Beaches: "Enough about me. Let's talk about you. What do *you* think of me?"

In my first book, *Revealing Riches and Building Lives*, it was mentioned that this is one of the primal challenges faced by church musicians. In order to be effective at teaching music, we simply must have a good grasp of our art and craft. We need to be professionals through and through. Having thus been hewn from the rock of classical musical performance—which is by definition self-focused—we are then called upon to enter a field of music *ministry* where the spotlight shifts dramatically to the needs and development of others. Singing like an angel is one process. Helping someone else to sing like an angel takes another set of abilities, insights, empathies, and skills. Great musicians are not necessarily great teachers, healthy role models, or inspiring mentors.

Is it even possible to move from such self-absorption into arenas where we become enablers, mentors, givers, and inspirers of others? The answer, of course, is a resounding yes! Who of us cannot name a quick dozen musical heroes who are at their very best when they're bringing out the finest in their students? I have names and faces of a few of my heroes flowing through my head right now: Andre Thomas, Cathy Britton, James Morrow, Jo Scurlock Dillard, Anton Armstrong, Michelle Roueché, David McCutchan, Larry Dickens, Gay Munselle, Eddie Airheart, Doug Jewett, Kimberly Clark, Jonathan Rodgers, and Robin Segarra, just to name a few. There are several hundred more.

Somehow, all of these stellar music educators have discovered linkages between their own gifts and the young women and men whose lives they intersect. For each of these directors, a creative spark mystically jumps from teacher to student. Each relationship they develop seems to hold a special synapse of its own. As a result, even mass groupings under these teachers' batons catch the chemistry, and the experiences ignite into magical musical moments.

How does this happen? How can Jo step in front of a group of high school students she has never seen and have them eating out of her hand in a matter of minutes? How does Anton guest conduct a mass rehearsal of collegiate singers and connect with them as if he's worked with them for four years? How is it that Cathy knows intuitively when one of her singers is having a bad day? How does Andre seem to turn anything that moves into a fresh and stunning teaching illustration?

There are many contributing factors and variables at work here. Frankly, some of it is gift and is thus as impossible to adequately describe as the charisma and charm of the Royal Family of Great Britain. However, there are several "ordinary" (though really extraordinary) factors that I believe contribute to the greatness of these and hundreds of other unnamed super-teachers.

- The conductor clearly knows what she is hoping to achieve with this group. She knows the music inside and out, and the musical goals—even the emotional aims—are clear to the conductor before she ever issues a downbeat.

- The conductor has a reputation of greatness and excellence preceding him. The students are anticipating a life-changing experience. They arrive on their toes, excited to be working with this well-known artist. This kind of initial credibility only comes with reputation over time.

- The conductor's skills are truly major league—engaging, clear, and clever, but also universal and understandable. This is a rare combination of technical prowess. True, some of what we observe is raw talent. But most of it is hard work, experience, and insight gained over decades of work.

- The conductor has an approach and background slightly different or even somewhat unique from anyone else on the planet. The students find this person somewhere between very interesting and highly intriguing.

- Although the master conductor may appear to be hard-wired in her approach, in reality she is constantly exercising flexibility, innovation, and creativity. From her massive repertoire of techniques, she is calling forth every tool she needs, custom-fitting each approach to bring out the best result from the group before her.

- The conductor becomes quickly transparent and real to the students on some appreciable level. She displays a contagious sense of humor from time to time and is able to have fun with the group—but never at the expense of anyone. She employs a rare and unique blending of intensity and relaxation. She becomes vulnerable and playful, perhaps poking a little fun at herself without coming across as self-deprecating or falsely humble.

- The conductor is obviously passionate about the rehearsal, and, at a handful of critical moments, he demonstrates that passion in a heightened level of expression. This does not mean losing control or going over the top, and it does not insinuate that every moment must be hard-driven. On the contrary, like a well-sung phrase, a rehearsal will have certain crescendos and apexes followed by sustained energy on the sweet sides/back sides of the phrases. In other words, the rehearsal itself has an effective tempo and rhythm, an hour-long sense of "macro-rubato." No two rehearsals feel exactly the same. Each session has its own personality and chemistry.

- The conductor fosters a rehearsal atmosphere where the musical learning is only a part of the whole experience.

- The conductor understands and celebrates music as a beautifully shaped tool, perfectly suited for the process of building richness, joy, and fulfillment in the lives of young people.

- The conductor realizes that it is not all about her.

- The conductor allows himself to fall in love with the group and learns how to express his affection in sincere and appropriate ways.

… we are to be lights in the world. It's God's business to light us, to set us on the lampstand, and to bring people into the house. Our only duty is to shine forth with the gospel.
– Marva Dawn

Take a deeper look at the list of conductor characteristics above. Each one of these qualities depends upon the leader being true to herself, understanding what her special gifts are, and being comfortable in her own skin. In a nutshell, here is what is happening:

> Diligence (intensive, lonely score study when no one is watching)
> Clarity of purpose
> Commitment to excellence

Talent given back to God as a gift to students
Craft developed and refined over decades
Uncanny flexibility and innovation
Distinctive or unique approach
Transparency
Humor
Good naturedness
Winsomeness
Vulnerability
Passion
Love
Affection
Self-control without being controlling
In touch with his own feelings without being psychologically manipulative
Open expression of deeper emotions
Sensitive and appropriate
Patient with pacing

The key to the list of qualities is authenticity. One thing is for sure: students have always been able to spot a fake a mile away, and millennial students can spot insincerity three miles away.

Beyond the long list above, there is a lifelong pursuit of beauty and an unending passion to bring that beauty into the experience of the student.

Outside the rehearsal, we have the opportunity to personally mentor a percentage of the students who sing in our choirs. Our mentoring must not become acts of favoritism, but rather our simple availability in response to the student's interest in knowing more or seeking help. No teacher/minister can provide any student unlimited access to her time, office hours, or professional space. However, much mentoring can be accomplished hour by hour in the seams separating the time compartments of our schedules. Many times, it only takes a moment for the spark of interest and care to jump between teacher and student. We must not underestimate the power of a glance, a friendly pat on the back, a smile, or just a quick, kind, and affirming word. Again, sincerity is the key, because millennial kids can detect glad-handing faster than they can sniff out a butyric acid stink bomb in chemistry class.

There can be no vulnerability without risk;
there can be no community without vulnerability;
there can be no peace, and ultimately no life,
without community.
—M. Scott Peck

At the beginning of this chapter, I mentioned that musicians can become notoriously self-absorbed. In addition, many of us are also very internally insecure. When we become aware of these insecurities and fears—more times than not deriving from our own childhoods and adolescence—we will do well to hunt them down, confront them, and give our best energies to working through them. Finding a good, caring counselor's couch can be good therapy for those of us who are regularly up in front of groups of students. We want to be sure we're whole and teaching healthy lessons (nonmusical as well as musical) every time we engage.

Who of us has not, at some point, gotten in front of a group and simultaneously gotten ourselves in a bind? I am thinking of a time (not nearly long enough ago) when I stood before a mass choir a thousand miles from home. I was fatigued to the core and distracted by several last-minute detail curve balls which threatened to derail eighteen months of planning. I was under unusually high family stress, and the last three weeks had seen several fifteen-hour workdays at YouthCUE. Musically, I was thoroughly prepared, but overall, I was not in good shape.

I might have seen it coming and called in one of my trusted colleagues to substitute for me but, frankly, it sneaked up on me. It happened so fast that I was blindsided and clobbered in the intersection of tight schedules.

Going into rehearsal, I nipped and snapped uncharacteristically at the students early on and got things off on a slippery footing. We got through the weekend, and I think some positive things happened. However, there were also some memories made that I would rather forget … and that I hope the students will be able to forget, forgive, or at least place into a larger perspective. I beat myself up for it for weeks afterward. I was not proud of a few moments of my nonmusical teaching that weekend.

Scott Peck's words above are true. There is risk in vulnerability. There is a certain danger in authenticity. Being *real* is not *really* a good thing if I am feeling *really* unkind or if I am *really* impatient. As a result of the less-than-stellar weekend, I was reminded once again that when teachers stand in front of students, the stakes are very high. It's not enough just to be real, and sheer transparency doesn't accomplish the larger goal of our work.

I suspect that, when we're honest, we all have learned such lessons through the years. Frankly, I hope we have all risked at least enough to fail in this regard. It is a humorous and humbling thing to realize that the conductor often has as much to learn on some level as the students standing before him.

But that's part of what makes this whole choral music thing so fascinating, fun, and fulfilling. I plan to stay with it, and I'm committed to becoming a better conductor, teacher, minister, and mentor with every passing year.

Join me?

> Vulnerability is the only authentic state…
> Don't mask or deny your vulnerability: it is your greatest asset.
> Be vulnerable: quake and shake in your boots with it.
> The new goodness that is coming to you,
> in the form of people, situations, and things,
> can only come to you when you are vulnerable, i.e., open.
> —Stephen Russell

Take It to the Next Level

For us directors:

1. On a scale of 1 to 5 (1 being the least, 5 being the most), how vulnerable and real do you perceive yourself to be to your students?

2. Is this where you want to be, or would you rather be closer to 5?

3. Is it a good idea to stay at 5 all the time?

4. Recall a time when 1) you were too vulnerable in front of your students, or 2) you wish you had been more careful before letting out negative feelings, or 3) the student actually reacted negatively to your "realness." As best you can, allow those feelings to return to you so you have a vivid memory of how it felt. How did the students feel? What did they express back to you, and how did they express it?

5. Knowing yourself as you do, what is the best way you can assure that you will find a good balance between authenticity and appropriateness in your leadership with students?

6. Who are your heroes in the arena of authenticity in leadership? Identify and list some of their leadership characteristics.

For the students we serve:

1. How well do you feel you know your youth choir director?

2. Would you like to know her better?

3. What would help you learn more about what makes your director tick?

4. Would you consider helping your choir director with some of his many leadership responsibilities with the choir?

Lesson Four
Time

Aren't you, like me, hoping that some person, thing,
or event will come along to give you
that final feeling of inner well-being you desire? Don't you often hope:
"May this book, idea, course, trip, job, country or relationship fulfill my deepest desire."
But as long as you are waiting for that mysterious moment,
you will go on running helter-skelter, always anxious and restless,
always lustful and angry, never fully satisfied.
You know that this is the compulsiveness that keeps us going and busy,
but at the same time makes us wonder
whether we are getting anywhere in the long run.
This is the way to spiritual exhaustion and burn-out.
This is the way to spiritual death.
—Henri J. M. Nouwen
Life of the Beloved: Spiritual Living in a Secular World

What do you consider a waste of time?

Before rushing to a quick answer or pronouncing swift judgment on video games, television, hockey season tickets, or fanatically following major league baseball, please read on. I ask all of us to hold off until we have at least considered the following lines, our lives, and the students we direct.

There are two stories in this chapter. Both are fictitious in that they do not represent any one person. On the other hand, they are true because they are composites of several people I have known, including myself. Perhaps these "people" and their stories can help all of us make better use of this, the most precious of life's commodities—our time.

Story 1—Addicted to Total Control

Jonathan, a music education major, was so driven that every minute of every day was meticulously scheduled. He kept an itinerary as tight as the President of the

United States, and the thought of wasting five minutes was utterly egregious to him. Jonathan graduated cum laude with his BME and later, upon completion of the MCM, he won a coveted graduate award for academic achievement. He gave serious consideration to beginning DMA work, but he decided he'd rather go from his masters directly into music ministry.

Soon after graduation, Jonathan accepted a demanding and promising church job and began pursuing it with all the time management skills he had perfected during his formal education. His ability to stay on track was indeed impressive. Church members and colleagues alike marveled at his discipline and the way he stayed passionately within his schedule. However, it was sometimes irritating to church members and teenagers whose issues did not fit into Jonathan's Daytimer. There were a number of students as well as adults and fellow staff members who would have loved to become better acquainted with Jonathan, but he never had time for any of them.

After about eighteen months, Jonathan hit a wall and felt the need to request a leave of absence from his church job "to get his life together." During those first couple of years of real world ministry, Jonathan had constantly tightened and ratcheted up his time management skills so he could fit more and more into his busy days. It had become a game with his music assistant to see just how much he could handle in short increments. People who needed him felt as if they were taking a number at the driver's license office and consequently were being handled as such.

Thus, after a year and a half, Jonathan began to feel something terrible deep inside. "I'm beginning to think that *my whole life* is a waste of time," he mused in despair. Having perfected the game of time management in "ministry," Jonathan had the sinking feeling that what he was doing may not be ministry at all. He began to consider other ways of living his life, using his time, and accomplishing his work, but he knew it would not be easy to change his old habits. He was, after all, already 28. This pattern of behavior had been going on since he was a senior in high school about a decade earlier.

With the help of a good counselor and the understanding ears of some close friends, Jon began to discover the insecurities from his childhood and adolescence that were driving him to this over-the-top obsession with time-management. Throughout the next several weeks, he was able to detox to some extent and begin working within a new frame of reference that included, among other things, being sensitive of others and their feelings.

One day, Jon said to his counselor, "I feel that I'm trying to recover from some kind of addiction."

"You *are* recovering from an addiction!" his coach responded stoutly. "It is entirely possible to become addicted to something that is basically good, but when it takes over your life, becomes the most important thing and squeezes out everything else, it's *not* good anymore."

Through the ensuing therapy, changes in behavior, and adjustments in lifestyle, Jon has not only survived, but he now thrives.

Today, over a decade later, Jon has found a workable balance in his life and work. He is married, and he and his wife have two beautiful daughters. Are there still challenges in time management? Of course there are! Is there still a tendency to give into the addiction of trying to control everything around him? Most certainly! But Jon is now aware of how important it is to strike good balances in life and work: raw time-management and sensitive ministry, work and play, intensity and relaxation, friendship and professionalism, relationships and achievement, family and church.

Story 2—Addicted to Fun

Everybody loves David.

What's not to love? He's winsome, hilariously funny, witty, smart, and gifted. He can carry on a conversation with a fence post and bring a smile to anyone with the faintest of a pulse. David has a big heart and genuinely cares about the people around him.

David bumped along through high school and was able to schmooze his way through the rough spots that came along. Flashing that million-dollar smile helped him navigate many a storm and even took him well up the ladder of peer leadership.

Upon entrance at the university, David declared himself a music major and registered for freshman theory. It was not long before he encountered his first collegiate nemesis: key signatures. It was the beginning of a long year which would be punctuated by arguments with the professor regarding the necessity of learning the rules of eighteenth century harmony.

"He's so intense!" he reported outside class, comically mocking the prof's perceived determination as he spoke. "Who needs this stuff? It doesn't even sound right, anyway! It's not the eighteenth century any more, is it … aren't we, like … three centuries beyond that? Maybe he'd be happy if I wore a powdered wig to class and spoke in King James."

You would have to admit that the animated diatribe was hilarious and, at times, David's friends experienced soda coming out their noses as the gang sat around the cafeteria guffawing. Unfortunately, the funnier David became, the more he withdrew from doing any of the required work. Somehow, David seemed to feel that enough laughs would surely have some positive effect in raising his final grades. The results of that kind of thinking are pretty easy to predict.

David tried to make it on his talent, good-looks, comedy, and charm. He could play the frets off a guitar, had a gorgeous tenor voice, and composed songs that should have been made famous by pop stars. David was an awesome and gifted performer. Perhaps that was the biggest problem; maybe he didn't need to be in music school after all. It is entirely possible that his real calling was on stage.

He was, however, determined to be a church musician and choral director ... that is, until the semester grades were posted. Eventually and painfully, David managed to scrape together enough hours to be called a sophomore before he completely dropped out. By then, the rest of us were nearly seniors.

Throughout his college career, David never made a to-do list, never carried a calendar, rarely thought beyond tomorrow, and seldom gave more than a glance to his studies. The bare necessities were usually completed with some degree of effort, but his grades were always marginal until the periodic exams inevitably did him in. Evenings were spent listening to music and strumming his guitar, going to campus sporting events, and playing video games. Coffee was consumed by the gallon, and it became harder and harder to make his 9:30 a.m. class on Tuesdays and Thursdays. All David's other classes were scheduled after lunch, which worked out well with his newfound propensity to sleep until noon.

David was never interested in anything that was not inherently fun. When the fun ended, he was outta there! True, there was a significant lack of discipline in David's life, but more than that, there was little or no commitment to anything which called for sacrifice, self-denial, or commitment to something bigger than just himself. Even with all the predictable hilarity surrounding David, his life was difficult to watch.

We could engineer and write a happy ending for David, but I am not sure we should. Being true to the composites from which this character was drawn, I am unsure of how the majority of these stories turn out.

We do know, however, that young men and women can grow up and amaze us with their development, maturity, and focus. We have seen this with our own eyes, and it is always fascinating to observe it when it happens. We shall hope and pray this happened in the case of David.

An additional possibility—Can David and Jonathan become friends?

If David and Jonathan had been classmates or roommates at the university, they could have been great for each other. Through friendship, communication, conversation, and understanding, the two could have been as close as David and Jonathan in the Old Testament. Close, yet different.

Sometimes, I feel that David and Jonathan are both at work inside me! No, I don't believe student choir directors are necessarily clinically schizophrenic or bipolar. I do believe, however, that we all do a certain amount of negotiating between two competing internal entities—the hard driven time-manager we have developed and the playful child who naturally wants to live life to its fullest and just have some fun. They both live and knock around inside most of us.

Rather than abuse and beat down one and completely turn the other loose, is it possible to nurture both, to treat both lovingly, and to develop enriching internal conversations between David and Jonathan?

I believe we can. I believe that, if we are to be at our best in ministries, we must!

Let us re-ask the original question: What do you consider a waste of time?

Even the Bible can confuse us if we quote passages out of context and try to take them literally, if not, at least seriously. Take a look at these seemingly conflicting scriptural instructions, which say in one place to be still, to rest and be quiet, and the next to work hard like an ant and not become a sluggard. Which is the waste of time, to rest and sleep or to continually work like an insect?

> See then that ye walk circumspectly, not as fools, but as wise, redeeming the time, because the days are evil. - *Ephesians 5:15-16*

> Be still, and know that I am God: I will be exalted among the heathen, I will be exalted in the earth. - *Psalm 46:10*

> For thus saith the Lord God, the Holy One of Israel; In returning and rest shall ye be saved; in quietness and in confidence shall be your strength: and ye would not. But ye said, No; for we will flee upon horses; therefore shall ye flee: and, We will ride upon the swift; therefore shall they that pursue you be swift. - *Isaiah 30:15-16*

> Yet a little sleep, a little slumber, a little folding of the hands to sleep: So shall thy poverty come as one that travelleth, and thy want as an armed man. - *Proverbs 6:10-11*

> And why take ye thought for raiment? Consider the lilies of the field, how they grow; they toil not, neither do they spin: And yet I say unto you, That even Solomon in all his glory was not arrayed like one of

these. Wherefore, if God so clothe the grass of the field, which today is, and tomorrow is cast into the oven, shall he not much more clothe you, O ye of little faith?—*Matthew 6:28-30*

My first thought was to assume that the Old Testament would command us to work hard and the New Testament would give us a graceful and merciful break. But that's not it, either. Both Testaments encourage us to both make the most of our opportunities and also to rest.

It's a matter of finding a holy balance in our lives, something that can occur only when David and Jonathan become friends.

In our student choirs and in our relationships with teenagers, it is important to realize that they, too, have a sense of what is time well-spent and what is wasted. Millennials have little patience with that which they consider wasted time and energy. They want to know, like the rest of us, that their investment is going to be of value in some significant way. Sometimes it will be necessary to educate young students about what is truly worthy of the investment of their time and talents. As we have discussed in earlier chapters, there will not always be an instant reward for the momentary investment. But taking a look at the long term, students can be taught to appreciate and even aspire to that which takes time to develop and appreciate.

In our choral rehearsals with students, it is imperative that we continually consider and evaluate issues of our preparation, pacing, time-efficiency, and energy. If you have been a YouthCUE reader for very long, you know that one of our criticisms of most rehearsals is that the director talks entirely too much. The constant flow of verbiage from directors normally is the result of a lack of preparation, vision, or purposefulness. The best choral rehearsals are, in and of themselves, works of time art, sketched out, designed, and fine-tuned to take the singers from where they are to where they need to be. This work of art will not be accomplished if we are shooting from the hip or walking in half-baked.

Remember, David and Jonathan can be friends in choir rehearsal settings, as well!

One last time, let's pose the question: What do you consider a waste of time?

Leisure, fun time can be wasteful, or it may be profitable. Hard work may can be constructive, but sometimes it reaches a point of diminishing returns.

So, how do you know what is a waste of time and what is a good use of this finite resource?

It depends more than anything upon the overall rhythm of our lives and how serious we are about making every moment count for the Kingdom. If we are committed to being a servant of the Lord and giving all we have as unto God, there will be no waste.

This is the longest chapter thus far in the book, meaning that it will take more ink to print, more trees for paper, and more minutes to read and digest. I hope it has been a good usage of your time!

Take It to the Next Level

For directors, let us consider the following:

1. How can I more effectively use my time to be a better disciple of Christ?

2. Do I need more play or more hard work and discipline?

3. Who do I know who can actively encourage me to be a better balanced Christian leader?

4. Is there a difference between "being still and knowing God is God" and doing nothing?

5. How will my life feel different when I find the balance I am seeking?

6. How will my life be impacted when I feel more fulfilled and at peace?

For the students under our care, let us ask them the same questions for their own lives.

Lesson Five
Organization

An idea can only become a reality
once it is broken down into organized, actionable elements.
—Scott Belsky

Becoming organized is much easier said than done. One of the reasons it is tricky business is because it is entirely possible to become totally organized and still miss the essence of down-to-earth ministry with students. Remember Jonathan in Lesson Four?

In a few instances, I have been called upon to provide counsel, consulting, and guidance for directors who have seemed to have it all together but whose programs were floundering mightily. If just being sufficiently organized were the only component required for student choir effectiveness, it might be a relatively easy ministry to pull off.

Routine is not organization, any more than paralysis is order.
—Arthur Helps

On the other hand, I have observed through the years a substantial number of programs that significantly lacked organization, but students were coming out of the woodwork to participate. Their parents made enormous sacrifices for them to be involved in these ministries because the choirs so radically impacted their teenagers' lives.

Go figure.

Why even write a lesson on organization if it seems to make such little difference in the overall outcome of a student choir?

Here is why: stronger, more excellent organization can help any program to better focus its efforts and more effectively utilize the available resources in order to become all it can be. Now that seems simple enough!

A schedule defends from chaos and whim. It is a net for catching days.
It is a scaffolding on which a worker can stand and labor
with both hands at a section of time.
— Annie Dillard

The catch is when the organization focuses on itself (the structural components) rather than the available resources at hand. Building a youth choir is not primarily about organization and structure. It is about effectively identifying, recruiting, engaging, utilizing, prompting, building, and celebrating all the available resources.

Furthermore, those resources are usually far more available at our fingertips than we dare to realize. It is easier to lament, "Well, I just don't have anything or anyone with whom to work." In 95% of all cases, such a statement is nonsense and is little more than an excuse for not digging in and working at it.

This is why some rather disorganized youth choirs work pretty well and some highly structured choirs never really get off the ground. The difference is what the director decides to do with the majority of his time … organize the program or build relationships with the students.

Given a choice of all one and zero of the other, I would have to choose relationship-building, because it is so utterly critical. However, there is no reason it has to be an either/or. It certainly can be a both/and.

The only things that evolve by themselves in an organization are
disorder, friction, and malperformance.
—Peter F. Drucker

Here is a theological question for you and me to consider as we think of the life of Christ and this whole question of organization: Was Jesus organized by today's standards … or by ancient standards, for that matter? To be sure, we know that God is a God of higher order (even routine, if we take into account the seasons of the year and the orbits of the planets).

But looking at God Incarnate, Jesus Christ, do we see evidence that he did his ministry in an organized fashion? Instead of WWJD (what would Jesus do?), we can ask HWJP (how would Jesus plan?). Did he put together organized efforts, or did he just take things as they came?

It is not our purpose in this lesson to fully answer that question … only to pose the question to cause all of us to consider it, perhaps for the first time. We might even reach different conclusions, and that is perfectly okay. But one thing that can be said for certain is this: whether "organized" or not, Jesus had a way of setting aside human schedules, expectations, and even religious calendars in order to reach out to hurting humanity. Jesus, being God's only begotten, can teach us a great deal about the place of schedules vs. reaching out in love— seemingly spontaneous love— to touch others.

Whether or not we determine that Jesus was organized in his ministry by Third Millennium standards, there is still no excuse for us not doing all we can to reach students with beautiful choral artistry and scripture-based music.

> *Once an organization loses its spirit of pioneering*
> *and rests on its early work, its progress stops.*
> —Thomas J. Watson, Sr.

I hope the following statements will prove helpful to all of us as we seek to be more effective in our ministries.

1. Organization and structure are helpful when they cause us to make sure we do all the important things in our lives: take care of ourselves, eat healthily, exercise, play, pray, read good books, meditate, commit scripture to memory, reach new students, make sure we engage and utilize their talents, remember their birthdays, congratulate them on the good things they are accomplishing, and be there when they are hurting.

2. Organization and structure as ends in themselves will leave directors very frustrated and unfulfilled.

3. Organization and structure can help the ministry to move ahead indefinitely, even outliving individual directors, pied pipers, and personality-driven choirs.

4. Organization and structure can never provide decent substitutes for joy, fun, goodwill, and team spirit within the choir.

5. Organization and structure are components—gifts—loving directors provide their choirs to assure each individual student is valued and treated as special, that no one falls through the cracks, and that the program can continue to thrive even when the director departs.

Want to get organized? Here are some basic suggestions.

1. Remember that good organization is organic. It is alive, ever developing, and always growing. We cannot do it exactly the same way over and over again if we expect the choir and individual students to grow and develop.

2. You and I as directors are not required to have the first, last, and middle words in our organizational structures. Remember, Thomas Jefferson did not write the Declaration of Independence all alone. He had the very active input of 55 colleagues who signed off on the document. Frankly, there may

be other people in our music ministries who are better equipped to provide leadership to the structure than we are! We will do well to encourage their gifts forward.

3. How can we tell if our organization is effective? If the job of ministry is getting done, the students are engaged, growing and developing and using their gifts, everyone has an opportunity to participate, and everyone is treated as the special gift of God that they are, than there is good reason to believe that your organizational structure is effective. If not, let us keep working on it. With God's help and the love and support of one another, we will get there. And when we do, it will be well worth every minute of time, effort, and organizational power.

The new organization is edgeless, permeable, amorphous ...
constantly re-forming according to need.
—Unknown

Take It to the Next Level

For directors to consider:

1. What elements of your student choir organization are working?

2. What parts of it are clearly not working?

3. Are your students involved enough in the organizational leadership of the choir? Too much? About the right amount?

4. What would it take to set up a revised organizational structure, or create a new one, that would be truly effective?

For students to consider:

1. How willing are you to become involved in helping your director become organized for success in your student choir?

2. Are you willing to really work at it, to make a commitment to give extra time and energy, to not just "hold an office" but to have a task to complete?

3. Can you see your choir reaching more students with all the good things your ministry can provide?

4. Would you be willing to invite a friend at school to be a part of the choir?

Lesson Six
Buzzwords

Growth in business occurs when a company figures out how to accomplish tasks faster, cheaper, and with fewer human errors. Businesses in general, and individual entrepreneurships in particular, develop specialized vocabularies to cut the froth and get right to the substance of high production and profit. Put that specialized vocabulary on steroids, ratchet up its effects, then abbreviate it, and the results are: buzzwords.

We have all heard some buzzwords, and we probably have some idea of what they mean:

Bottom line – the actual end result

Urban Amish – city dweller with no cell phone, no laptop, no iPod, no Blackberry

Go up-line – move it up the chain of command

Team player – do we need to even define this? It is usually stated in the negative when it is not happening … "not a team player."

Money-out – makes sense financially, makes a profit or meets financial goal

Reinventing the flat tire – making the same mistake as before even after much debate and a formal vote

Results-oriented – hard-driven and is willing to put financial results ahead of people's feelings

Fund-drainer – an event that loses money for the nonprofit organization

News snackers – those who get their news in very short bursts from sources such as Twitter, RSS feeds, mobile phones, and glimpses of TVs posted on gas pumps or in elevators. As in most snacks, they are very tasty, but they are not very healthy over the long term.

> *OT mail* – an unnecessary, unproductive email sent to supervisors and co-workers afterhours for the simple purpose of time-stamping how late you worked

Business does not have a monopoly on buzzwords, however, and there is certainly no shortage of them in ministry. This chapter will take a close look at three of our more prominent buzzwords in youth choir ministry. As in all buzzwords, their primary disadvantage is that they over-stereotype and force large groups into narrow categories. Let us take a closer look and see what we might learn.

Relevant

Some church leaders now use this term as a sort of litmus test or Holy Grail for programming. The question is often asked in inquisition form, in pressurized ways to evaluate the viability of certain church programming and ministry.

"Is this really relevant?"

Immediately, those put on the spot by the question begin to fidget and figure ways to defend why the programs they lead are "relevant." What is most interesting is that, when the question is flung out for immediate and simple response, the background questions are seldom addressed.

"Relevant?" Yes, that's a fair question.

"Relevant to exactly what?"

"Relevant to whom?"

"Relevant to what ends?"

These are better, more complete questions, although they do not fully plumb the depths of what needs to be addressed.

How can we determine if something is relevant if we are not clear what it is we are trying to do? What are we seeking to achieve? With whom are we seeking to achieve it?

Over what period of time are we going to evaluate the results: over the next week, next month, the next year, or over the next decade?

In what cultures are we seeking to be relevant, to what groups of people?

In order for us to be truly *relevant*, do we not also have to be *reliable*?

In youth choirs, in order for an anthem to be relevant, doesn't it also need to be rehearse-able? In other words, doesn't it need to be a piece of music we can build upon and discover deeper meaning as we practice it?

Let me ask a question that probes even deeper: Is it more important to be relevant or revolutionary? If we are truly revolutionary, the changes we make will tend to be permanent. If we are content simply to be "relevant," we will likely be flip-flopping programmatically with every passing year.

Is it important that our ministry be reusable? In other words, will we be able to build tomorrow upon the ministry we place in front of our students today? Will we be able to build upon it next year and ten years from now? Shallow "relevance" as it is normally used may not pass the test of re-usability.

Are the messages and texts we put forth in our program actually true? Are we content to hit just the "relevant" high spots of the gospel to the point that its presentation is actually skewed, shallow, and shifting?

Is what we're doing with students simply "what's hot?"

Does our ministry make a difference in two worlds?

Let us take a look at some words and phrases to determine if these are "relevant" or not. And remember, we always have to ask the question: "… relevant to what, relevant to whom, relevant to which cultures, and relevant over what period of time?" Here is the list:

> English literature: relevant or irrelevant?
>
> World history: relevant or irrelevant?
>
> The NBA: relevant or irrelevant?
>
> Word-crafting and writing: relevant or irrelevant?
>
> Dance: relevant or irrelevant?
>
> Ice hockey: relevant or irrelevant?
>
> Pipe organ: relevant or irrelevant?
>
> Dallas Cowboy Cheerleaders: relevant or irrelevant?
>
> Baroque music: relevant or irrelevant?
>
> Abercrombie and Fitch: relevant or irrelevant?
>
> The Book of Psalms: relevant or irrelevant?

To be sure, we can put together a very quick list of what's hot and what's not. Are we, in our ministries, using "relevant" as synonymous with "popular?" I believe many of us may have fallen into that trap.

If so, let us be honest and name it for what it is: popularity, marketing, and sales quotas. But there is no call to attach the Savior's name to it. Why do we, in the name of the Lord, claim one-dimensional relevance or irrelevance based upon today's popular opinion? Is it our calling to rush to our students' whims about what is "cool" and what is not?

What kind of schools would we have, and what kind of foundation would our students receive from public education if we allowed teenagers to choose their own curriculum? What would happen if we disposed of all syllabi which did not pass our 16-year-olds' short-sighted tests for "relevance?" It would certainly become a darker world, and it would do so in short order.

The key to subject matter becoming relevant is the skill, ability, and passion of the teacher to inspire and impart life-lessons to the students. The reason why so many youth choir leaders opt for shallow "relevance," better known as popularity, is because oftentimes we, as a guild, lack the ability and commitment to build the relationships and teach the deeper lessons. It is much easier and less costly just to hit the high spots and move on. Alas, the high price for such shallow ministry is paid by the students themselves. The best youth choir ministers among us are those who know how to teach teenagers and are willing to walk with them through the difficult days of adolescence.

That is a picture of true relevance—relevance in action.

Millennials

Every seventy years or so, there is a generation born which ultimately changes the world. The millennials are that generation.

Born between the years 1983 and 2002 (some say between 1981 and 2000), this generation is like none other we have seen. Here are some of their characteristics:

- Millennials are the most racially and ethnically diverse generation in history.
- Millennials are, as a group, the most politically progressive generation in modern history.
- Millennials have grown up with high technology and it tends to come naturally to them.
- Millennials are the least religiously observant group since religious behavior has been charted.
- Millennials are more trusting of institutions than the previous two generations.
- Millennials are more tolerant and celebrative of diversity than previous generations.

- Millennials tend to view other people by what they can contribute than by age or cultural markers.

- Millennials view technology and social networking as a natural way to gather their world views.

- Millennials often possess intuition and innate ability with technological devices, which is best compared to perfect pitch in music.

- Millennials view "membership" as an irrelevant concept, unless "membership" produces or provides something special.

- Millennials are motivated by self-actualization—maximizing the expression and results of talents, passions, abilities.

- Millennials' generational "currency" is as much about time as money.

- Millennials view "Control," "Corporation," "Company," and "Church" as curse words when they stifle creativity, passion, and honesty.

- Millennials possess over-the-top ability to translate concepts, ideas, and programs into technological expressions.

- Millennials develop and process ground-breaking relationship-building within social networking.

- Millennials are able, as no previous generation, to bond with individuals and groups across the world who share common views, philosophies, and passions.

- Millennials will preside over a society which has the capacity to divide and/or unite as never before. Peacemaking will require a new level of creativity and integrity.

- Millennials have already discovered that, with information overload becoming an ever-increasing phenomenon, finding truth and identifying integrity will be dependent more upon healthy relationships and a strong internal compass.

Millenials respond well to structure and will follow good leadership and guidance. Since millennials are often ready to take on the world, they need encouragement of their confidence and can-do attitude. Millenials often work well on teams and can find fulfillment working together.

Make no mistake about it, millennials have the upper hand. Whereas those in older generations may have knowledge, experience, and wisdom, the millennials are unique in that they understand more fully how to communicate these qualities through technology and media.

In business, this means that the fifty-five-year-old may have produced and perfected the product, but without the millennial's mind and talents, the older person will be hampered in seeking to sell his particular commodity.

In ministry, it indicates that old, young, and middle-aged need to work together intergenerationally to bring the message of Christ to the world. The good news is that millennials have no problem with that. They do not generally see generation gaps and, remember, they tend to accept people more readily for who they are, respecting others for what they can contribute to the whole. They also tend to work well in groups. As long as millennials are able to express their creativity and "have a life," meaning time to pursue things other than work, they tend to be very productive.

At the beginning of this chapter, we made note that buzzwords often tend to overgeneralize large groups of people and fail to take into account productive individual differences. As we engage, befriend, and minister with millennials, it is important to realize that the classic, crucial stages of adolescence are also at work for these students until they mature. We will do well and minister more effectively if we realize that each student, regardless of his or her generational designation, is a unique and beautiful person in the eyes of the Creator.

Let us heed the broad category called "millenials," but let us also look beyond the general label to see deeper into the soul of each student!

Legacy

In a quickly-advancing world, those of us in ministry have realized there is no guarantee that what we put in place today will stand the test of time. Just because a ministry is hammered down firmly during our tenures, we can never be certain that it will be here a decade from now. Many factors contribute to this uncertainty and, fortunately, there are also many ways to anchor good work and give it a fighting chance for survival beyond our tenures.

First, we must be intentional. If a youth choir is worth sending into the future for success and innovation, directors need to be thinking beyond what we will sing at Christmas or where the next mission trip will take us. We must take a longer look into the future, dream, and work our plans backwards from what we hope the group will eventually achieve.

Second, we must realize that we are but one stone in the wall. We may be the greatest student choir director of all times, but we will not be in this place forever! Our ministry will come to an end one day. For some, those types of future thoughts are depressing "downers," but for many of us, we are actually energized to consider how our ministry may live long after we are gone. In order for legacy to be realized, we simply must come to terms with our own temporariness, indeed, our own mortality. Many churches, upon retirement of longtime pastors, have suffered immeasurably because the minister simply could not let go. It's painful to observe. It's even more painful to live through.

Third, the dream we leave needs to be more about positive attitudes, openness, and innovation than about programming in a certain way. We make a mistake when we try to fashion actual programs that become sacred cows and traditional bulwarks over many decades. When we do that, we tend to build our ministries with our personalities at the center, making ourselves the center of this ministry universe. The tradition we should hope to pass down would be one of clarity of purpose.

Fourth, realize that God's work takes on many forms, progresses in ways we might not previously imagine, and is not dependent upon me for survival. It can be tough on our egos to realize that the world will go on without us. It will be a better place when we're gone if we have been faithful to develop leadership in other people, particularly in those who are younger than ourselves.

Finally, the millennial generation—now in full bloom in our student choirs—is perfectly primed and ready for friend-making, mentoring, leadership development, and carrying on the legacy. The only question left to answer is: how much are we willing to invest in this generation? No amount of investment and time will be too much. It will be worth every ounce of energy we give and every minute we spend!

Lesson Seven
Text

Holy words long preserved for our walk in this world,
They resound with God's own heart; O let the ancient words impart.
Words of life, words of hope give us strength, help us cope;
In this world where'er we roam, God's ancient words will guide us home.
—Lynn DeShazo
From the song *Ancient Words*

How important is the text in youth choral music?

One of the clear pictures we can paint to point out the importance of text is the image of nutrition.

How vital is it for kids to grow up partaking of nourishment more substantial than cotton candy, chicken nuggets, fries, candy bars, and soda? Most of us parents have had to work long and hard to get our toddlers-turned-children-turned-adolescents-turned-young adults to try some healthier foods than what naturally strikes their appetite fancy. For some kids, it's a harder job than it is for others. But difficult or not to achieve, a healthy diet is a priority good parents cannot ignore.

When left strictly to their own desires and choices, few kids will ever learn to eat right, at least not until some damage has been done to their bodies with too much sugar, cholesterol, and fat. Somehow, poor eating habits normally seem to partner with inactive lifestyles. The overall effect is not difficult to predict. When we are not eating healthily and we don't feel as well, it's more of a chore to get up off the couch or away from the television, computer, or Xbox.

Perhaps the cycle of bad eating, low activity, and poor health can be broken in a number of ways. Most people, when active with regular exercise, tend to crave healthier foods. It's the body's way of taking care of itself and building up strength and endurance.

Before coming on too much like a health magazine, let's find our way back to student choirs. With the image of nutrition fresh in our minds, let's discuss the texts we choose for our teenagers to sing. The connection between the two is not a long leap, but a short hop.

Time-Honored Text

The best parents among us are those who are able to help kids get what they need more than what they want. The trick here is that the kid himself usually doesn't know what he needs or what he's likely to need in the future. Furthermore, as consumerism has run its rampant tsunami over this generation, many kids don't even really know what they *want*. As adults, we have a little more experience with those needs and desires than those in the younger generation.

"Hey, this isn't *school*," many well-meaning parents sometimes communicate to youth choir directors. A good response could be, "No, it is not school; but what we do here is as important to your child's spiritual development as school is to her intellectual advancement. Simply giving teenagers what they want at church is tantamount to allowing a teenager to quit school when it ceases to be all-out fun and games."

Put it all together, and it is obvious that the texts teenagers sing are more important than most of us realize. Obviously, scripture texts memorized in an anthem are going to remain deeply embedded in teenagers' hearts and lives for decades to come. There is no gift greater than providing students timeless scriptures scrolled upon the walls of their awareness for time and eternity.

At the writing of this book, we have just completed YouthCUE's Seventh Annual Baylor Festival of Youth Choirs. This festival is unlike any of our other major festivals because we have such a high level of repeat traffic. Several choirs have been there all seven years, and some have even changed directors in that period of time. At the Seventh Annual Festival, we had our first crop of high school seniors who had participated in every Baylor Festival since they were in sixth grade.

Think of it for a moment. Each Festival features ten anthems, almost all of which are straight scripture (the rest are normally prayers, hymn texts, or classic poetry). Ten anthems per year, multiplied by seven years—that's seventy sacred choral anthems these seniors have memorized during their middle school and high school years. Taking just the texts they have memorized, they have committed to memory what would be equal to approximately a dozen to fifteen chapters of scripture. Is there anywhere besides youth choir where students will quote that much scripture from memory? Moreover, the scripture memorized is set to music, which makes its memory all the more firm, on the tip of the tongue, and embedded in the heart for time and eternity.

At YouthCUE, we continue to hear the stories by the hundreds. Teenagers, now well into their college years, adulthood, and parenthood, report that at key, pivotal times in their lives—or just driving down the freeway—a passage (anthem text) comes clearly into their minds, reminding them of the providence, love, and grace of God. It has saved some from suicide in critical moments. It has enriched everyone who has sung.

Thankfully, there is currently a myriad of wonderful music available for today's directors of student choirs. Hundreds of these anthems have, at their core, the incomparable word of the Lord.

As directors and their youth choirs give themselves to the pursuit of powerful scripture texts, the energy flows in from every direction. Many directors, upon turning to scripture texts, have reported an almost overnight choral transition for the good. Rehearsals become alive, energized, and full of new meaning. Vitality rushes like a raging river. The overall mission of the choir—to lead worship for the congregation and to serve others outside the congregation—begins to make sense and flourish inside and out. Through scripture, the students begin to get it and discover that they were created for a purpose.

Text-Honored Time

Nothing can put life into perspective like scripture. Nothing can speak to us with utter relevance and power like the potent passages of the Bible. As youth choir directors, there is no better use of our time and energy in the musical setting than to incorporate and integrate scripture with gorgeous and exciting choral sounds.

Do you want to make absolutely certain that you are not wasting the kids' time in rehearsal? Feed your choir scripture through the anthems you set before them. The time you spend with your students in that environment will pay eternal dividends not only now, but particularly in the future.

Timely Texts for Whatever Is Next

None of us knows specifically what tomorrow holds. However, there are some things we can know with assurance about the future. Today's teenagers are going to grow up and face crises in relationships, health, career, family, marriage, finances, and in some cases, all of the above and more. There will be good times as well as episodes of loss, grief, and stress. We need not wonder about these things, but rather, we must help students make the investments which will keep them sane, healthy, functional, and growing during the spiritual challenges. You and I share an enormous responsibility and privilege in this arena.

However, those of us who have been at it a while also recognize that the fulfillment and joy we share with our students and now grown-ups are veritable tastes of heaven. Is it easy? Seldom! Is it sometimes discouraging? Absolutely! Is it worth the high price we pay for it? Without a doubt, it is!

The texts we impart to teenagers, particularly to the older high schoolers, will begin to affirm and sustain them much sooner than we might imagine. Whatever life throws at them, they will find meaning and joy and hope, because scripture teaches us that Christ will never leave us or forsake us.

It is our privilege and joy to provide teenagers with that good news, to embody the truth in every move we make, and to reinforce the love of God with every word we sing.

Take It to the Next Level

For directors to ponder:

1. Consider some of the anthems you are currently using which are scripture settings. Recite a few of these texts aloud. Ponder what these texts are communicating to your students.

2. Is there anything in your current repertoire list that is "a textual waste?" In other words, is it of little value or even worthless theologically?

3. What anthems (whether or not in your current repertoire) do you feel are some of the finest musical settings of particular scripture texts?

For our students:

1. Which anthems mean the most to you from your total youth choir experience—including those from previous years?

2. Discuss why these anthems are so important to you.

Lesson Eight
Road Trip Momentum

One of the beauties of a choir tour is that we get to come home! At first, that might sound a bit crass—assuming the tour experience was not fun for the director, or a sort of endurance contest. But this is not what we are seeking to convey. One of the great things about a choir tour is that we are able to bring home the benefits of the work we have begun with our students while on the trip!

For sure, some things, indeed some very positive things, can happen on a choir mission trip which will never happen at home. There is a certain chemistry connected with a road trip, being away from the home environment, focusing on a worthy team project, having some needed space from certain friends and the healthy company of others. A trip is a unique opportunity for relationship-building, for self-discovery, for new commitments. In a word, a good road trip is a special time for … ministry. The blessings we seek to bestow upon those we meet in our mission projects will always come back to "out-bless" our groups and our individual teenagers.

We directors sometimes make the common mistake of focusing our major energy on the seniors, those who have just graduated and are on their final tour. Although it is important to provide a special memory or two for these outgoing leaders, it is equally important to concentrate on building the relationships that are the future of the student choir. The future begins only a month from now as we begin new youth choir years!

In the new, upcoming season of singing, caring directors can find ways to build upon the following tour accomplishments with the returning kids:

Directors who engage with their kids gain needed insights and discover valuable raw information. I cannot tell you the number of times I have sat beside a teenager on a bus ride and have heard "the story of his life." By being a decent listener and asking a few good questions, I discover data points that soon provide extremely valuable insight into this kid's home, his interests, his dreams, his dreads, his hopes and fears. These points of raw information provide the gateway into healthy mentoring.

New friendships and deepened relationships develop. A director who makes her way to different parts of the bus will find herself quickly getting to know her students. These one-on-one vignettes and small group encounters can become a huge resource for directors in the coming weeks and months. A tour can launch fulfilling relationships between directors and students, between students and students, and between students and adult counselors.

A student's level of spirituality, maturity, and commitment will often be unveiled during trips. Some of the most profound theological discussions I enjoy take place during choir road trips. It is important that we allow these young neophyte followers of Jesus (aren't we all?) the space and acceptance to pose their questions, to expose their view of the mystery of God, to honestly wrestle with issues for which there are no quick, easy answers. We make a serious mistake with teenagers when we feel called to constantly "set them straight," to quell their curiosity about the nature of God, or to be too quick to jump in with "the right answer" to what they initiate with us. We must always remember that adolescence is a time of floating test balloons and expanding horizons. So often, the "issue" being discussed is not "the issue" at all in the teenager's mind. Many times with kids, the test balloon they are floating is a red herring question to see what the response is going to be from us. Some kids delight in throwing forth outlandish concepts just to see if we will still accept them and love them, weird ideas and all. If we pass the test of providing unconditional love, most kids experience a diminished need to be "so far out there." We often discover that we, the adults, are the ones being put to the test, and the exam has little or nothing to do with being spiritually superior or theologically above reproach. For us adults, the test question, though almost always silent, is "Would you still love me even if I completely rejected your value system?"

So … will you?

Will I?

Will we?

Leadership is blossoming before our very eyes. With every passing year, there is a new crop of leaders coming forward. "Wow, I wish that were the case, but I just can't see it with this group of young kids." Spotting leadership-in-the-making takes not only careful observation; sometimes it requires a modicum of holy imagination, as well. The only leaders we will develop are the ones we can imagine becoming leaders. If we can't imagine a kid emerging into a leadership role, there's no way we can help him cross the threshold from bench-warmer to play-maker.

New choir officer elections. Whether you refer to your student leadership team as officers, steering committee, or … the student leadership team! … the end of tour is a great time to elect new leaders. There are a variety of ways this can be accomplished, and each group seems to function best in its own style and system. As you elect your leaders, consider giving yourself the power to appoint some of those who should be/could be leaders but do not make the popular vote. Experience shows that there will be only a few raw-material leaders who are not selected by their peers, but there are almost always exceptions to the rule.

With some prayerful thought and consideration, you and I can bring the benefits of choir tour back home, invest those returns into the future, and build the leaders we so desperately need! We waste valuable time and energy if we are just planning road trips for our student choirs. Far more productive—and yes, more fun—for everyone involved is an adventure in leadership building.

Say "road trip" to a group of students, and everyone is ready to roll! Just the thought of getting out of town, away from home, and in the company of close friends is enough to ignite the energy and imagination of most teenagers for months at a time. This is particularly true if there is a history of good travel experience in the group's tradition of ministry.

As exciting, fun-filled, and happy as road trips can be, they can also be designed to provide crucial nurturing which is very capable of strengthening the spiritual fabric of every participant. When we directors determine to develop leadership as a part of our travels, the ministry opportunities flow through our choirs like rich fountains of youth.

There is a myth among youth groups and youth choirs that only the older teenagers—and perhaps the super-gifted "middle aged" ones—are the only students who are capable of giving leadership to a group of their peers. The fact is, every person in your youth choir possesses some form of leadership ability, some potential for greatness that needs only to be discovered, encouraged, nurtured, and developed.

It begins with thinking outside the box. Obviously, the kid who is an outstanding musician, a born leader, a superb verbal communicator, or who has a winsome personality will naturally gain our initial attention. Teenagers blessed with natural good-looks and gregarious personalities tend to be the first on our list of leadership recruits. But history has proved that some of the best leaders in our society, churches, government, and industry were late bloomers. Because they did not have the great looks or the outgoing personalities early in their lives, they have had to work hard to achieve what they have accomplished. Their leadership blossoms later than that of their peers, and it often lasts much longer.

In years of ministry with a wide range of teenagers, the gamut of personalities, and a huge array of gifts, I have to admit that many have greatly surprised me. I have actually been shocked on both sides of the coin … how little some gifted teenagers failed to accomplish as adults, and how much some "average" kids were able to amount to in their college years and beyond. If you have been involved with teenagers for any length of time, I know you could share similar stories of both disappointment and delight.

We encourage all of us to take a fresh look at our developing, growing, and maturing groups of teenager in our care. Instead of just traveling with them, let us build an exciting adventure that will unearth and reveal our students' leadership potential. Let us set their lives on a trajectory of service to others and excellence in all they do.

Simple Ways a Mission Trip Can Begin to Build Leadership among Teens

1. *Submit required paperwork by deadline.* It's important that the students themselves be responsible for getting in their forms, payments, and paperwork by deadline. Encourage parents NOT to take care of this for their "children."

2. *Write thank-you notes.* To supportive home church members, to hosts at mission projects, to anyone who helped and contributed to make the trip successful.

3. *Serve on specific work force.* Students need specific tasks to complete as a part of a team: bus cleanup, luggage coordinators, and work coordinators.

4. *Reach out in mission projects.* It is one thing to be a part of a mission project; it's another to actually reach out and personally touch a person in need.

5. *Mentor younger teenagers in the group.* There are dozens of innovative ways this can be accomplished. Creatively connect older teens with younger.

•••

She took a seat beside me on the bus and offered to get me a Diet Coke out of the nearby icebox. Slowly downing our drinks, she began to talk, this senior in the final days of her final youth choir tour.

"Randy, this has all meant so much to me," she said with tears brimming up in her eyes. "I can't believe the past six years have gone by so fast, and, here I am, at the end of my Celebration Singers experience."

"I know," I responded, smiling and gently shaking my head east and west, then north and south. "It's amazing how quickly time escapes us. And I'm sorry to break it to you, but it just keeps getting faster. Before you can turn around twice, you'll be a college junior and then headed off to graduate school. So, what's been your favorite part of this whole youth choir experience?"

"It's all been good," she said, her eyes drying out a little. "The whole thing: all the worship services, the Chamber Concerts, the mission projects. They've all been great. But the one thing that has meant the most to me has been these trips. There's something about the way you plan these things that make them just so incredibly special and meaningful. We've been to Seattle, Minneapolis, Denver, New York, Washington, D.C., North Carolina, and Florida. But the strange thing is this: as we've gone far, far away from home on these tours, the feeling I always get is that when we go on tour, I'm not *leaving* home, but I'm *going* home. Tour feels like home to me. When we finally drive back into the parking lot at church on the last night of tour, that's when I feel that I'm going back into a strange world."

I sat silently looking deep into her eyes. I was taken aback, because I must admit, in all my years of directing youth choirs, I had never heard that perception expressed that clearly. "Tell me more about that," I said.

"Well, my friends know that my home hasn't always been the happiest place for me during my high school years. There's just so much … so much garbage and emotional baggage to work through with my parents and their expectations and all their … their … their *stuff*. Every day is a new struggle. Conflict is at every turn. I don't know. They just seem so … so *dysfunctional* or something."

I was still a little stunned by what I was hearing, but I'm not sure why I should have been surprised. I tried to engage her a little more. "Sarah, I'm feeling a couple of emotions as you talk. First, I'm so glad that we've been able to be here for you. And you've been here for us, too, because you've made a huge contribution to this group. Secondly, I'm feeling sad because I'm so sorry that your family hasn't been able to provide you the security you've needed. I know your parents, and I know they love you very much."

"I know they've tried really hard," she interrupted. "They have done the best they can, but there's just so much bad history in their relationship. It's really sad."

We sat silent for a moment and watched the scenery go by outside the huge bus window.

I slowly patted her hand, and said, "Sarah, you know you don't have to repeat the same scenario when you fall in love, get married and have your own children. It can be different for you—very different—and you can break the cycle you have experienced. You can become anyone you choose to be."

"I know," she said. "Because of Celebration Singers, I have a fighting chance at doing something different for my kids. Thanks!"

"Thank *you*!"

"I love you!"

"And I love you, too!"

Several fellow seniors then called Sarah to the back of the bus, where a new game of hearts was being dealt on the top of an Igloo.

Today, over ten years later, I remain Facebook friends with Sarah and her husband, who now have a beautiful two-year-old daughter. They live in a city five hundred miles from her hometown. They are thriving and making a strong contribution to the church and community in which they live. They recently came and visited us at a YouthCUE event in their city.

· ·

So, fellow directors, would you say our hard work is worth it or not?

Take It to the Next Level

For directors, ask yourself the following questions:

1. Have there been times you have taken your choir on the road and you have realized, mid-tour, that good things were happening which could not have happened at home? Think back and get in touch with that time, those happenings, and those feelings. Describe it.

2. What have been the overall benefits of the time you have spent on the road with your students? Answer the question for your choir as a whole, for individual students, and also for yourself.

3. What do you hope to give your students in future road-trips?

For students, respond to the following:

1. Describe your favorite road trip with your choir.

2. What made the adventure so special?

3. Who were the people in your group who stood out to you as the best leaders? What impressed you about them?

Lesson Nine
Compassion

How far you go in life depends on you being tender with the young,
compassionate with the aged, sympathetic with the striving,
and tolerant of the weak and the strong.
Someday in life, you yourself will have been all of these.
— George Washington Carver

Whether in ministry, public service, at home, at school, on the highway, in the courtroom, in a youth choir rehearsal, or on a working mission trip, the heart and art of compassion must be constantly and carefully taught to our young. The Apostle Paul in 1 Corinthians 13 states it about as clearly as anyone could. He gives us a powerful, unforgettable bottom line for our lives and our service. "Without love, I am nothing."

Too often we underestimate the power of a touch, a smile,
a kind word, a listening ear, an honest compliment,
or the smallest act of caring,
all of which have the potential to turn a life around.
—Leo Buscaglia

You have already discovered that the pages of this book are punctuated by powerful quotes regarding human compassion. Our greatest leaders in all walks of life have known from the beginning and had it reinforced over time: compassion, empathy, and kindness are the key components to abundant life and human joy. Notice, we did not say "human happiness."

One should never direct people towards happiness,
because happiness too is an idol of the market-place.
One should direct them towards mutual affection.
A beast gnawing at its prey can be happy too, but only human beings
can feel affection for each other, and this is the highest achievement they can aspire to.
—Aleksandr Solzhenitsyn

It is a rather strange thing to note that empathy, although having huge and global implications, begins with the smallest of things. Instances such as these:

I am in a huge hurry in the overcrowded grocery store at 9:45 p.m. In the middle of the aisle where I need to go is a mom trying to do her shopping with four small children in tow. They seem to have everything blocked up in several aisles. My first thought is, "Why aren't those kids home in bed where they belong at this hour? What crazy mother would drag her kids out at this hour for a trip to the grocery store?" What I do not know is that this mom and her husband, the kids' dad, have just moved to the City from 1,600 miles away. The dad works at FedEx and doesn't get off work until 1 a.m., and the mom herself just got off work at 7 p.m. when she rushed to daycare to pick up her children, has fed them dinner, and this is the only time she has to do grocery shopping. Husband and wife are adjusting to new jobs, the kids are trying to make new friends both at school and at daycare afterwards, and this family is just trying to survive the first month in a new city. What do you think? Are these folks deserving of some compassion, or should I just write them off as idiots as I scurry by, popping a wheelie with my shopping cart?

Showing some compassion when our waiter at Cracker Barrel seats us at an awkward table, makes a couple of small mistakes with our order, lets our iced tea glasses sit empty for five minutes too long, and then makes us wait an extra minute or two to receive our check so we can pay out. My thoughts revolve around an ongoing critique of this obviously incompetent, unfocused waitperson. I issue several private slams on the young guy for being less than adequate, less than attentive to his customers. What I don't realize is that the twenty-something has received a phone call within the hour saying that, if he wants to see his grandfather alive, he had better leave work as soon as he can find a replacement and get to the hospital ASAP. Granddaddy, this young man's major mentor and support system in life, has just had a massive stroke and will probably only make it another few hours. Would it be good to cut some slack to this young fellow struggling to make it to the hospital in time to say goodbye to his best friend?

Giving a break to the old woman on the highway who is driving too slowly and has several vehicles backed up behind her in her lane. As people pass her, they turn and glare as if they are looking at an axe murderer. She is in the slow lane and there are still three others, but we are convinced this woman should NOT be on the road. It's unbelievable. She should be arrested. What we have no way of realizing is that this seventy-five-year-old lady with slightly diminished eyesight is headed to the hospital to do her weekly volunteer work among pediatric cancer patients. Normally, her younger sister drives her to work and picks her up at the end of the day, but her sister is at home today with the stomach flu. Knowing that this was a big day at the hospital and several volunteers are out sick, the lady decided she could get herself to work if she left early and just took her time on the highway. She was careful to stay in the slow-moving lane and she did a superb job of keeping her vehicle under control, but that was not good enough for those who were determined to fly by, driving fifteen to twenty miles an hour over the speed limit. Should this volunteer among children's cancer patients be awarded a modicum of understanding and patience, considering her situation?

Human compassion on a global scale is somewhat worthless if we can't find empathy for the person ahead of us in the ATM line, next to us on the interstate, or trying to find a parking place at Walmart. What good is it to be globally caring if we're locally caustic, personally cold, and provincially brutal?

> *I would rather feel compassion than know the meaning of it.*
> —Thomas Aquinas

Having a go-go-go attitude toward life, always pushing ahead, constantly driving forward at breakneck paces—these ultimately work against the heart and art of compassion. To develop compassion during adolescence, students must be encouraged to stop and think beyond their own desires and their own perceived momentary needs. When we dare to slow down, to stop, and to move our attention in another person's direction, compassion has a place to begin.

> *We who lived in concentration camps can remember the men*
> *who walked through the huts comforting others,*
> *giving away their last piece of bread. They may have been few in number,*
> *but they offer sufficient proof that everything can be taken from a man*
> *but one thing: the last of the human freedoms—*
> *to choose one's attitude in any given set of circumstances,*
> *to choose one's own way.*
> — *Viktor Frankl*

As directors of student choirs, we are engaged in the heavenly task of teaching compassion through the music we conduct and the life's lessons we provide. Whether leading worship on a Sunday morning, singing in a prison or nursing home, performing hands-on mission projects for the disenfranchised, building a house for a needy family, painting walls for the Salvation Army—we have the opportunity to open the flow of compassion in the young women and men we serve. May we do it all, with our own unique brand of love and empathy, with divine love, which initially derives from the heart of God.

> *Nobody has ever measured, not even poets, how much a heart can hold.*
> —Zelda Fitzgerald

There is no greater calling than to unveil in students' lives the treasure-trove of compassion within them. Every rehearsal we hold, every measure we sing, every text we memorize, and every life we touch can reveal to them and foster in them compassion and love of Christ.

We frail humans are at one time capable of the greatest good and,
at the same time, capable of the greatest evil.
Change will only come about when each of us takes up
the daily struggle ourselves to be more forgiving, compassionate,
loving, and above all joyful in the knowledge that,
by some miracle of grace, we can change
as those around us can change too.
—Mairead Maguire

Take It to the Next Level

For directors, consider the following:

1. How have I sought to convey the spirit of compassion to the students in my choir?

2. How has the choir responded to the challenge to develop its sense of compassion?

3. Have there been individual students who have stood out among their peers as being especially caring and compassionate? Describe these students.

For students, think about the following:

1. How has our choir shown genuine compassion through its ministry?

2. How can we do a better job of giving in the community immediately surrounding the church?

3. What anthems are we currently singing which remind us to develop Christian compassion?

Lesson Ten
Entrepreneurial Spirit

In the new millennium, the truly dynamic,
community-changing churches and ministries among us
are going to have to learn to become
more entrepreneurial and less custodial.
—George Mason

The quote above was first delivered in 1988 to an audience of budding ministers. At the time, it had the ring of a prophetic word about it, but not many of us understood what entrepreneurism would look like within a local church.

Although unclear about the word "entrepreneurial," most of us in the room already had a clear and colorful idea of what "custodial" meant. Even as early as 1988, many of us young ministers had already gotten a belly full of custodial-style thinking and programming.

Take a look at what dictionary.com has to say about these two words:

en-tre-pre-neur *noun*
1. a person who organizes and manages any enterprise, especially a business, usually with considerable initiative and risk.
2. an employer of productive labor; a contractor

cus-to-di-an *noun*
1. a person who has custody; keeper; guardian.
2. a person entrusted with guarding or maintaining a property.

It is interesting, just from the wording of the two definitions themselves, how one employs action verbs and the other indicates more of a static state of being. One is dynamic; the other is stagnant. One takes energy; the other demands comfort. One looks forward; the other looks back.

The entrepreneur organizes, manages, initiates, risks, produces, employs, and contracts.

The custodian "has" stuff: trust, guardianship, maintenance, custody, facilities, property.

In the new millennium, custodial programming consists of drawing a circle around ourselves, fencing in our facilities, and protecting the favorite cows that have now become sacred. It means maintaining schedules, regularly dusting all that we have, developing carefully-worded policies, and normalizing procedures and actions so no one becomes upset. It insinuates taking no chances with money, people, or other resources. It calls for playing it safe and eliminating the risk to less than a 5% chance of failure. Being a custodian means finding that magical sweet spot in our planning where we can all relax together and never have to worry again about having our comfort zones rattled, shaken, or God forbid, torn down to make way for something better.

Entrepreneurial ministry is not just a little different from custodial programming; rather, it is foundationally different at the cellular level. In the entrepreneur's DNA there is always found a gene of risk taking. There is a fearlessness of long hours and hard work. There is a burning passion to make the world a better place. There is an inextinguishable vision of diverse people working together to accomplish something truly special for the communities and worlds around them.

Entrepreneurs are sometimes seen as gamblers. In the world's eyes, that's what risk is—betting, rolling the dice, gaming, gambling. In the faithful Christian's heart, however, risk-taking is synonymous with expressing visceral faith in an ever-faithful God, who not only calls people to do special tasks but also empowers them with everything they need to get the job done.

Custodians. Entrepreneurs. Is there any way to get these two people to become friends?

George Mason was absolutely right and, at YouthCUE, we see proof of it every day. Unfortunately, those student choirs bent on custodial-style programming are languishing in all kinds of churches across the land—in small towns and large cities, in mainline denominations as well as nondenominational models, in upper class neighborhoods as well as inner-city slums.

On the other hand, entrepreneurial directors and their innovative choirs are flourishing in a colorful variety of settings across the world.

Difficulty develops when the director is forward-thinking, entrepreneurial, and innovative, but the church he serves is not. Over the years, we at YouthCUE have known a number of directors who were virtual lone rangers in their churches. Several were seeking to develop youth choir ministries in their churches with little or no support from their fellow staff members, congregation, or existing students.

Why swim so hard upstream against such an ominous current? In each case, these directors possessed a burning passion to see their students experience the benefits of a strong youth choir ministry.

Reality is that some churches provide little more than a losing battle for directors who long to provide choral music for kids. In most of these cases, the staff simply does not get it, does not share a vision for choral music. In others, the contemporary element has gone to seed in the congregation to the point that choral music has been relegated into the category of "irrelevant."

How does a caring director survive and live out her vocation when there is no value assigned to what she longs to provide?

What follows is not so much an answer as it is a series of soul-searching questions. Through the honest addressing of these questions, perhaps we can uncover new possibility-thinking for the years to come.

In our lifetimes, we have seen in some places the custodial approach to church give way to more creative partnerships, innovative programming, and cutting edge ministries designed for people rather than for the perpetuation of a traditional program.

The first question: Is it possible that some youth choir programs in some communities need to happen outside the four walls of the church?

In such cases, there is sometimes simply not enough room in the church's already packed programming to accommodate this thing called youth choir. Is it possible to think of creating a strong choral ministry with teenagers in the community and outside the four walls of the church?

The second question: Even though such ventures might not be known as "church youth choirs," can't they still connect into the worship of local churches and still concentrate on choral music of the Christian faith?

When you think about it objectively, could we not imagine an innovative scenario where several dozen students from nearby churches combine to form a strong choral community? As far as we at YouthCUE can tell, the reason this does not happen more often is because of an ancient, twentieth-century territorialism among church communities. When this happens, the students suffer the most, but everyone loses. Not only are we drawing lines between our congregations, but we are also narrowing the students' range of musical expression. Without meaning to do so, we communicate to them that unless they sing in contemporary style and can be a praise and worship leader, there is no place for them to engage musically.

The more we see and hear, the more convinced we become that the answer may lie in building choral ministries free of the preconceived and narrow views of some existing church music ministries. These groups need not stay outside the church. They could be brought back into the communities of faith for periodic worship leadership across denominational lines.

Community choirs that are following this general model tend to provide broad-stroke support and overall strength for the youth ministries in the individual churches they represent.

Obviously, combining non-cooperating groups will produce a fiasco. But compatible partners who are not resistant to stretching a little administratively for the sake of their students could become very strong forces of bridge-building within their communities.

It most certainly takes an entrepreneur to begin a community youth choir, but it also takes an innovator to grow a student choir in a traditional church setting. Perhaps the former takes more courage, again referring to the element of risk mentioned earlier in the chapter.

The key to either community choir or church student choir is a dynamic director and staff who understand teenagers, can relate to them in kindness and gentleness, will take a calculated risk, will raise needed support, and develop a glorious vision for what can happen. Many areas of the country, from rural to suburban to inner city, are primed, ripe, and ready for a musician-entrepreneur with vision to move in and begin working. Areas where there is an absence of strong public school music are the most fertile fields for cultivation.

In conclusion, it is important to mention that the purpose of this chapter is not to remove a youth choir from the church family which values it. In a perfect world, every church that wanted a strong youth choir would have one, would highly value it, and would strongly support it.

Nor is the purpose of this chapter to try to reconstruct something in the community which the local church is trying to retain, develop, and build.

We are seeking to help youth choirs not only survive but thrive as they relate both to their churches and to their larger communities. In some locations, it is possible that the only way a youth choir can happen would be to have its organization and entrepreneurial roots out from under the shadow of the steeple.

It is our hope and prayer that the tribe of entrepreneurial directors will continue to grow and flourish, for indeed, the fields are white unto harvest.

Take It to the Next Level

For directors to ponder:

1. Can you ever see yourself directing a community youth choir?

2. If not, why not?

3. If so, what are likely to be the most significant hurdles?

4. Do you know anyone personally who is presently operating a community youth choir?

For our students:

1. What advantages, if any, would there be to being a part of a community youth choir?

2. Do you have friends currently not involved in their churches who might be a part of a community student choir?

3. What is the smallest number you could have in this choir and still be considered successful?

4. How large do you think it might become someday?

Personal Diagnostics no. 1

Is the pace of your student choir rehearsal too slow?

Planning and pacing our rehearsals will, to a great extent, determine the success and effectiveness of our entire student choir ministries. Woe be unto us—and our students—if the tempo of the rehearsal ever causes the time to be viewed as boring among the participating singers. A slow, dirge-like pace in rehearsal is the kiss of death.

The following questions provide a way of evaluating our effectiveness in pacing our weekly youth choir rehearsals:

1. *How many anthems do you cover—or at least touch—during one rehearsal?* YouthCUE suggests in a sixty-minute rehearsal that as many as ten anthems be included—either rehearsed hard, sung through for memory, or excerpted for particular phrase work. If your answer is less than five anthems, you may find yourself in trouble over the long haul. Teenagers can become bored and listless with the same old anthems, even if they can't sing them … especially if they can't sing them!

2. *What do you do if the rehearsal just seems to bog down on a piece of music, frustrating the students and throwing the director into uncertainty about how to proceed?* There is a time to push through, and there is a time to toss the piece aside for today and pick it up another time. This tossing aside cannot happen on the same anthem more than a couple of times, however, or the singers will develop such negativity towards the piece that they may never be able to conquer it. Section rehearsals are a great solution here, sometimes introducing tougher anthems through section rehearsals for a few weeks before they are ever brought to the whole choir.

3. *How much talking do you do?* One sure way to find out is to record your rehearsals and then go back and actually time how much you talk. When I have done this exercise in my rehearsals, I have been absolutely shocked at how much I talk. Please be very careful with this. Nothing will kill a rehearsal faster than too much sermonizing, or talking more than singing. Keep talk to a minimum; this applies to conductor as well as singers.

4. *How much time do you spend helping your accompanist?* We know it's true; no choir can go any further than its accompanist can take them. If we are spending even a couple of minutes at rehearsal helping the accompanist with her part or even correcting notes and rhythms, it will spell disaster in the loft. The accompanist must be prepared and on your team, helping to teach, rather than on their team, trying to learn the notes and rhythms.

5. *Does your rehearsal begin on time?* Believe it or not, this is one of the most dependable signs indicating the effectiveness of our pacing. If we begin on time, we tend to hit a better pace from the very first note we sing.

6. *Does your rehearsal end on time?* Keeping the students overtime in rehearsal is damaging to the pacing of the next rehearsal. If it happens too often, there will be a sense of laziness which falls over the group. After all, "He's going to hold us late anyway, so why try to learn in record time?" We must begin and end on time—even end early if at all possible.

7. *How animated are you in rehearsal?* A director glued to his/her music stand, watching every note go by, is sure to lose the students. Keep strong eye contact and move away from the music stand as much as possible. Unhooking from the score from time to time will also encourage the students to watch you and begin memorizing earlier.

8. *How long do you pray?* Yes, it is a great thing for the students to hear their director pray for them, and every week is not too much. What is too much is when the director preaches a sermon during his prayer. Over the past decade I have noted that teenagers tend to be quieter during the prayer times, even when I go on too long. Perhaps this shows the need for students to be still and quiet for their spiritual and emotional health. Or maybe it means they have fallen asleep!

9. *Does your choir ever move physically?* Several excellent directors in the YouthCUE network keep their students moving on a regular basis throughout the rehearsal. Take them to another part of the Sanctuary, go down the hallway to a more acoustically alive room. On a beautiful day, do the rehearsal under an outdoor covered walkway. Keep it interesting.

10. *Do you "hold court" following rehearsal?* Strange as it may seem, if the teenagers know they will have full access to their director following the rehearsal, it will have a positive effect upon the pacing of the rehearsal. Give them enough attention before and after the rehearsal, and they will be more attentive during your fast-paced practicing.

Personal Diagnostics no. 2

An organizational checklist for beginning a great season

1. Spend one hour evaluating the past season. Make lists of what was good and what needs improvement and innovation. Be as specific as possible about what worked and what did not. Do not overthink; this is why we suggest one hour. Move ahead to the next part of the process.

2. Take half a day. Go somewhere alone to be quiet, think, and pray specifically about your youth choir ministry—what it needs and what needs to happen. Take your list with you, and ponder anew—and alone—what the Almighty can do.

3. Communicate with your leadership team(s). Whether your decision-making group is comprised of youth, adults, or a combination of both, you need their input now. Use your best skills as a team leader, building consensus and not allowing the time spent to become a wandering, roaming idea session.

4. Gain clearance from the pastoral ministry team. Any kind of major initiative, specific dates, projects, trips, fund-raising—anything major and anything calendared—must gain the approval and the blessing of the pastoral team. The philosophy which says, "I'll seek forgiveness after the fact rather than permission beforehand" is a dangerous and potentially deadly proposition when dealing with youth choir ministries, particularly in multiple staff situations.

5. Put it on paper, preferably in detailed schedule form. Allow this document to be a major piece in the communication puzzle. Work hard at it and make it look professional.

6. Gather all needed musical resources … now! This means ordering the coming season's anthems in plenty of time for them to be placed in the youth choir folders in the days preceding the first rehearsal. A freshly-prepared packet of music that includes mostly new anthems with a couple of favorite oldies—this communicates volumes to the students when they arrive to begin the new choir season. We must be ready. If there are to be demon-

stration CDs or recordings to help you teach the music, these must be ordered and moving toward your office.

7. Invite every student in your church to join youth choir, even if they've turned you down several times. Summer is a great time to gather groups large and small for a soda, a swim party, movie night, or a glow-in-the-dark bowling expedition. Make these events outreach oriented with soft-sell invitations to become involved when the choir season launches. If you already have your program together for the coming year, this is great motivation for teenagers who are considering joining. The invitations we provide students can be official snail mail mailings, personal handwritten notes, phone calls, text messages, Facebook invitations, recruitment parties—the sky's the limit for creative and positive ways to engage kids. What is common to all these approaches is this: the more personally involved the director, the stronger the draw.

8. Plan a jumpstart event for early in the season. A retreat (overnight is best, but a day retreat is okay, too) can be a superb way to kick off your choir season. The objectives of such an event are to get a jump on:
   a. getting the students connected to each other, to the director, to the program.
   b. teaching a bunch of notes early, using section rehearsals, master classes, creative approaches.
   c. orientation to the season, what's expected, specific scheduling, plans for the year, announcing big events and summer schedule.

9. Give your best effort to giving the group a quick feeling of success. Clearly stated, don't wait too long before you provide your teenagers a singing venue for worship, a mission project, or some other special event. The group need not sing a lot of music, but it is important that they do well and feel good about their contribution to the program in which they are participating. From the beginning of the planning process, determine when the group needs to sing, and then stay with the plan. Remember, coaches have games scheduled before practices ever begin; they know they are going to have to field a team, ready or not. We directors and our students need the same type of motivation by schedule.

10. If possible, go ahead and order tee shirts for your group. An attractive yet cool-looking tee shirt can be one of the easiest ways to bring some unity to your group. By creating some visual togetherness, we are helping the choir become a unit functioning as a whole. I learned this several years ago when I attended freshman orientation for one of the large high schools in

San Antonio, a school which has a nationally-recognized band program. Even a week before school began, the band was there at the assembly, surrounding the audience and playing beautifully, all from memory, all wearing simple white tee shirts with a colorful logo over the left pocket. They wore the tees with jeans and tennies. They looked and sounded great, and school had not even begun yet. Psychologically, this was a strong statement to everyone, including to the band itself!

11. While registering your teenagers for youth choir, get a snapshot photo of each student, much like a photo ID. A person on the leadership team can easily be prepared to take a photo of each member (phone photos are fine) for use in a variety of ways. First, the director can begin to put names and faces together. Second, there's no reason a choir directory cannot be made available to everyone in the group. Third, the photos, along with names, schools attended, etc … can be placed on a bulletin board near the rehearsal area. You will be able to think of more appropriate and helpful usages of the photos in the coming weeks.

12. Once the program gets underway, it is essential that we stay in touch with our choir, especially the new members. We need to be in regular communication through text message, Facebook, or even through a regularly updated website.

Personal Diagnostics no. 3

What does it take to sustain a strong beginning?

The first rule is this: there needs to be something to sustain!

Not long ago, I became aware of a recently-hired church education minister who had arrived at his new job with more good ideas than you can imagine! But he wasn't just a dreamer. This guy had plans, seemingly solid plans, and it seemed pretty apparent that his strategies were going to work, and work big! What nobody anticipated, however, was that he made little effort—some say no effort at all—to gain the trust, relationships, friendships, and goodwill of the people he was trying to lead and, who were also, incidentally, paying his salary. He charged ahead into the fray without helping his army properly prepare. Heavy on the religious lingo and fluent in all the latest buzz-words, he assumed that all the credibility he needed was inherited with his hiring. After all, when God's on your side, who needs other people's opinions, right?

Is there any doubt about how this chapter ended? Suffice it to say it was an unmitigated disaster and caused much embarrassment for everyone involved.

The first rule in sustaining the momentum of a good beginning is this: *have* a beginning, work to build trust, and gain some positive momentum with the whole team.

Second, we need not be shocked or dismayed when the initial energy of any movement begins to slip back a bit, to normalize back toward status quo. This is certainly nothing to fear, but it is a reality that needs timely attention, even before the inevitable happens. When there is the initial energy loss, it is not necessary to hit the people with a dozen new ideas ... or even one, for that matter! What is needed is getting back to the basics, continuing to plan the future, and working consistently according to the plan. This is when it's crucial that we do all we do exceedingly well.

Tom Peters, in his book, *In Pursuit of Wow!* states that the truly effective leaders among us are not the ones who do extraordinary things, but rather those who do ordinary things in extraordinary ways. This is a vitally important concept. Doing ordinary things extraordinarily well implies great self-discipline, patient hard work, and implicit trust in the Power higher than ourselves to "provide the increase."

Thus, the second rule of sustaining the effects of a great beginning is: work diligently, discipline yourself to stay with it, and work at it long enough for it to really excel. Even the most talented leader needs time to perfect his plan in a new place.

Third, turn your back on quick fixes, silver bullets, wars to end all wars, and fountains of youth. If you have been in the ministry for a while, you know that there is no shortage in the availability of ecclesiastical snake oil and those who seek to wholesale it.

With regard to quick fixes, consider that the gospel of Jesus Christ is based upon relationships, and there is no shortcut to building healthy, long-lasting friendships and trust.

Regarding silver bullets, please remember that, although every one of us wants to be successful and increase participation in our ministries, we need to also understand that cancer is a growth as well. In fact, physiologically and biologically, it is a growth run totally amok, out of control, and insanely fast. It doesn't know how, when, or where to stop, so it ends up eating the whole organism, eventually ending in death. The cancer literally consumes itself, because as the terminally-ill cancer patient succumbs, so does the disease which has taken over the body. How insidious and evil is that?

In wars to end all wars, quick, cheap, and easy fixes are just that—quick, cheap, and easy. Their effectiveness over the long haul is as poor an investment as purchasing the absolutely cheapest set of tires in town. They will not stand up to the test of wear and tear and time. We'll soon be back in the tire store looking for a newer, cheaper set … that is, until we learn better.

With the current fixation on the exploitation of youth, remember that Moses, the stutterer, was eighty years old when God called him to lead the Hebrews out of bondage. So much for the requirement of a youthful appearance and the trappings of coolness as prerequisites for effective Christian ministry!

Personal Diagnostics no. 4

Before your first rehearsal of the new season, remember this:

Each time you and I begin a new youth choir season, it is a brand new opportunity, providing fresh starts and a clean slate with the teenagers you and I serve. It is a beautiful gift to us directors, this new beginning! We are allowed to bring virtually every positive aspect of last year into the present, while, at the same time, leaving some of the undesirable baggage behind. It is this continual purifying process that can make youth choir such a dynamic force in the lives of teenagers as they—and we—grow, develop, and mature.

Remembrance 1—First impressions are huge, so it is essential that we have our organizational acts together before that first rehearsal.

Remembrance 2—In the student choir arena, we are providing teenagers a combined set of experiences, encounters, and opportunities they can find nowhere else in their worlds.

Remembrance 3—The students need the respect of the adults around them, and the adults need the energy and "youth" of the students.

Remembrance 4—Adolescents can spot a fake a mile away. This is not at all to suggest that you and I are phonies, but it is important to understand that honesty and openness are essential in all our dealings with students. Kids' emotions are often so sensitive that even a careless one-liner or off-handed remark can cause misunderstanding and hurt feelings. To be sure, it takes a good deal of energy to stay on our toes when working with students.

Remembrance 5—Our youth choir is not so much the church of the future as it is the church in present tense. In fact, if our students are not learning how to be church now, how can we expect them to magically become the church ten or twenty years from now?

Remembrance 6—Students show up at choir rehearsal for a wide variety of reasons. Some are there strictly because it is a convenient and popular gathering place for them and their friends. Some want to make great music. Others want to be where the action is. Still others are seeking the security and acceptance of a loving group. And the majority is motivated by some unique combination of all of the above. Furthermore, even individual teenagers' personal attractions may change from one week to the next. What does this say to us directors? It says that the atmosphere and feeling of the rehearsal time is crucially important. We do well to give time, energy, and creativity in our attempts to make each rehearsal a warm, friendly place to be.

Remembrance 7—"The grass withers and the flower fades, but the word of the Lord is the same forever." When we sing scripture, we are giving teenagers a gift for eternity.

Remembrance 8—In work with students, success breeds more success and failure breeds more failure. Although we cannot control the outcome of all that we do, wise directors will do all we can to make the initial experiences of youth choir successful, fulfilling ones.

Remembrance 9—A large part of what we plant in teenagers' lives will not bear its full fruit until today's pre-adults are well beyond our immediate sphere of influence. The most beautiful flowers will bloom in the college years and beyond.

Personal Diagnostics no. 5

What do my students need from me as youth choir director?

1. A friend who gives unconditional love and acceptance.
2. A musician who is competent, comfortable, and creative in the choral setting.
3. A leader who keeps his promises.
4. A minister who is not short-fused or temperamental.
5. An organizer who cares enough to plan thoroughly.
6. A coach who knows how to motivate individuals as well as the team.
7. A counselor who understands teenagers and their emotions.
8. A theologian who provides spiritual guidance without being overbearing.
9. A self-disciplinarian who comes into rehearsal prepared.
10. A recruiter who encourages participation without guilt trips.
11. An artist who can connect kids with beauty.
12. A mentor who will model a mature, fulfilling life in Christ.
13. An educator who loves to learn as well as to teach.
14. An entrepreneur who makes the choir experience far-reaching and fun.
15. A travel guide who introduces students to new parts of the world.

Since all of us are human, none of us will live up to all these qualities at all times. However, we can take on this list rather effectively if we will read it from time to time and meditate on how we have succeeded or failed. This list can act as a personal prayer guide for ourselves as we consider the many facets of our ministries with students.

Personal Diagnostics no. 6

Giving students the gift of our personal time

None of us would argue the value of quality time given to teenagers as they cross our paths. However, as good as the concept sounds, what can directors actually do in practical ways to help provide the gifts of time and attention? How can we order our lives in such a way that we will become better ministers and givers of our personal attention?

It would not be a bad idea to grade ourselves from time to time and evaluate how we are doing with these goals.

1. Look the teenager in the eye when you are in conversation. Stop all other motions you have going on—music sorting, gathering up pencils, shaking other people's hands, whatever. Stop and look the student in the pupils of the eye. Watch and listen.

2. Speak to every kid you pass in the hallway, Sanctuary, classroom, or parking lot. Whether you know the student or not, smile and warmly greet this special adolescent.

3. Where appropriate, make appropriate physical contact with the teenager. Notice the word "appropriate" is used twice … three times now … to describe how we touch kids. There are good ways and bad ways of doing this, and when in doubt, simply refrain. Handshakes, high-fives, fist bumps, a pat on the shoulder, a light hug are generally good ways of relating to kids who know us well and place well-founded trust in us.

4. When a student visits your choir, he or she gets a hand-written note from you in the middle of that very week.

5. Facebook is a great way to "be friends" and keep up with your students who have Facebook pages.

6. Refrain from the temptation to "fix" the teenager every time you are around him. There may be teachable moments which will present themselves from time to time, but teenagers are really looking for someone just to listen to their feelings, opinions, and desires. Simple self-expression is a huge need

among teenagers, and we help them more than we realize when we provide a safe, accepting place for them to express themselves.

7. Let your choir hear you pray for them in rehearsals. Our ministry of prayer is a priestly function on their behalf, and our prayers can be more meaningful than any lectures we might deliver. Let me offer a word of caution, however: keep the spoken prayers to a reasonable length, because too much in this area will actually affect your rehearsal pacing and attendance. Generally, be concise, caring, compassionate, and emotionally connected to the kids as you pray for them. They will come to be still and will actually look forward to this time when offered up with sincerity and love.

8. Be comical. This does not mean we have to be comedians at all times, but directors who use appropriate, sharp wit with the students usually communicate well with them.

9. Go into their Sunday School departments from time to time just to be there and enjoy their company. Don't promote anything; don't actively recruit, don't try to put the moves on anyone to join choir. Just be there, be friendly, and smile a lot.

10. Speak in terms of the students' needs. This is an old Dale Carnegie principle that generally says: Talk about what the other person wants to talk about, and I will add that it probably will not be about music. Generally care about the students, whether they ever sing a note in your choir or not. Most will respond openly to your friendship when they sense that you care about them as people.

11. At your rehearsals, have your preparation done early so YOU can visit with the students as they arrive. Show a genuine interest in each one, and don't forget to reach out to the extra shy kid.

12. Likewise, if at all possible, be available at the end of rehearsal for questions, conversations, and personal affirmation.

Personal Diagnostics no. 7

A conducting mini-clinic for student choir directors

Experts in communication tell us that 85% of all communication is accomplished in the realm of the nonverbal. This reality has enormous implications for speakers, preachers, teachers, and musicians, to name only a few professionals.

Choral conductors should find the 85% rule a fascinating concept, because for musicians in ensemble, conducting becomes the ultimate nonverbal language.

What follows is a do-it-yourself clinic for choral conductors, whether aspiring or seasoned. These are simple, back-to-the-basics concepts which need occasional reminder for all of us. Practice, improve, and enjoy!

Few of us outgrow the need to practice in front of a mirror. Videoing our conducting is also a good way to help ourselves become clearer, more precise, and more expressive. I send all my young students to full-length mirrors to become self-aware and to help pinpoint areas where improvement is needed. Even after thirty years past my master's degree, I still benefit greatly from a session or two in front of my own mirror. I actually find the mirror to be more effective than video, because I can see issues immediately and address them right then and there.

Yes, the easiest and most effective do-it-yourself conducting therapy is in front of a mirror. By watching yourself conduct, both to recorded music and to silent, internal music, you will find glitches in your style that distract and need improvement.

Feet—Feet should be positioned as for a good singing position, approximately eighteen inches apart with one foot slightly ahead of the other, not in line. Weight should generally be shifted to the ball of the foot, occasionally shifting which foot is forward and which foot bears the most weight.

Never succumb to the temptation of patting your foot to the beat. In order to practice, "nail your foot to the floor," and refuse to tap your toe. All the energy for the beat needs to be transferred upward into your hands and fingers, not "leaking out" through various joints, such as ankles. For some directors, who have fallen into the bad habit of toe-tapping, being able to cure this problem will be a big accomplishment and thus an enormous improvement.

Here is a simple suggestion which simplifies and amplifies the suggestions above. Making certain that your feet are kept still on the floor, practice "sending upward" all the rhythmic energy you normally would feel in your feet. Transfer all that rhythmic impulse and beat all the way up your leg, through your torso, through your arms and into the tip of your index finger. Now, conduct a simple pattern with ALL the rhythmic energy focused on the tip of your finger. Keep practicing and do not allow your foot to tap. Placing a baton in your student's right hand helps to move the beat to the proper place. If using a baton, the beat must be at the tip of the baton, not anywhere else.

Legs—Work to relax the legs, particularly the calves and thighs. When we fail to do this—or when a seasoned conductor has an unusually long or difficult rehearsal and knowingly tenses his legs—muscular fatigue, soreness, and even cramps are likely to follow. Relax your legs!

Torso and shoulders—A singer's position is the rule of thumb for torso and shoulders. Everything here is held comfortably high and relaxed, never strained. A straight posture is essential. We often observe conductors hunched forward over their music stands, able to make eye contact with their singers only by raising their eyebrows and looking from a chin-down position. In many cases, the shoulders are held too high and rigid. The conducting pattern is sometimes generally too high, which causes the conductor's stance to collapse upon itself. Although the shoulders are held too high, it's also possible to slump.

In order to get started in the right way, stand with your back up against a wall. Stand tall but relaxed. Take two steps away from the wall and maintain the stance without becoming rigid. Take a deep, relaxing breath (a singer's breath or "cleansing breath") without raising your shoulders. If standing with good posture, you are already in a correct position for diaphragmatic breathing. Once you have relaxed a bit and have taken a couple of breaths, slowly bring your arms up and hold your hands side by side, approximately twelve inches from the tip of your nose. Make certain your chin is comfortably high without feeling stretched. Now, conduct a gentle pattern or two, but do not drop your eyes or your chin. Stay high. Relax and float a bit. Keep your conducting motions buoyant and fluid. Remember, no foot tapping!

Arms—By "arms" I am referring to everything from your torso to your wrists and excluding your hands. The arms—particularly the elbow—provide some of the greatest challenges in removing ticks, clicks, kicks, and glitches (all nonmusical terms simply meaning "false beats" or "junk movement") which throw off the real beat you are trying to establish. Your mirror and video camera will catch many "false moves" which subconsciously confuse your desired nonverbal communication with the musicians. Be especially sure that the real beat does not migrate from where it should be (hand and/or fingers) into the wrist, elbow, shoulder, hips, knees, or ankles. These are common mistakes made by young, inexperienced conductors as well as seasoned veterans who have not watched themselves in a while.

Hand and fingers—For the purpose of this exercise, the focus of the beat should be on the tip of the index finger. Think of the old (ancient?) movie, *E. T.*, when the extraterrestrial's pointer finger was lighted and glowing as he reached out to touch and heal his little friend's wound. With your index finger (or baton point) extended and "glowing," conduct a series of patterns very cleanly and clearly. No bumps, no hitches, no kicks … just simple and smooth movements which flow without jerks. Smooth! Legato!

Keeping the pattern clean—As conductors, our constant point of reference is a clean, clear, and simple pattern which can be followed by both singers and instrumentalists alike.

For many years, there was a definite distinction made between choral and instrumental conducting. When working with a strictly choral conductor, instrumentalists and even professional orchestras tended to fall apart because they could not find simple beat patterns in the choral conductor's gestures. At the same time, strictly instrumental conductors were no more popular with choral groups than were choral conductors with orchestras. The criticism with instrumental conductors was that they were too clinical and did not "get it" in terms of choral phrasing and sculpting of lines.

Thankfully, we have come to realize that great conducting is great conducting, whether the music happens to be choral or instrumental or a combination of both. Certainly, there are shades and nuances of difference between instrumental and choral styles, but neither should be so foreign as to confuse, frustrate, or upset the other. When executed well and with clarity, cleanliness, and precision, musicians of virtually any background can follow. If music is the universal language, then conducting is the universal, nonverbal language within music. Glorious conducting truly is nonverbal communication at its apex, the epitome of sign language.

Conducting is both science and art, both athletic and mental, both surface and psychological, both physical and spiritual, both motor and mystical. When done well, it will take everything you have to give to it, including the continual commitment and desire to improve. As singers and instrumentalists are encouraged to respond to our gestures and signs, they too can provide much-needed input for the improvement and perfection of our craft.

May we all keep practicing, improving, and becoming!

Personal Diagnostics no. 8

How can I overcome inertia?

Got inertia?

No respecter of age, race, cultural background, talent, ability, or educational level, inertia—the comfortable form of laziness or thoughtless perpetual motion—is rampant in the land. It thrives like an undiscovered tumor in our profession and spreads like kudzu through pews, choir lofts, committee meetings, and congregations. It is so subtle that even "church growth" can become one sinister form of under-the-radar inertia.

Anything that keeps us from taking the next needed step forward in our lives or communities of faith—that is inertia. If not checked, it can grow and metastasize, closely aligning itself with human evil. Out of fear, fatigue, faithlessness, denial, or simple failure to act upon the obvious, we stall, mark time, or simply pretend the next step has not sufficiently revealed itself. Famous slogans for the indefinite continuance of inertia include: let's wait and see; we don't want to rush into anything here; maybe if we ignore it long enough it will go away; I'll drag my feet on this to buy some time so maybe I'll won't have to deal with it; if I keep really quiet, perhaps no one will notice the rhinoceros in the room.

What is the next step you know you need to take? It may be as simple as committing to walk a mile a day or as complicated as switching careers or dealing with an addiction. For the majority of us (though not for all of us), that next step is probably located somewhere closer to the midpoint of the continuum. It's going to be harder than walking a mile a day, but it will not be as difficult as facing addiction and looking it in the eye.

What happens when we do not take the next step, when we at least temporarily succumb to inertia? Eventually, if we continue to remain in our lukewarm womb, a personal price of some significance will be paid. It may be a secret exacting, but it will be costly just the same. But that's not all. We not only pay inertia tax, but we also accrue penalties and interest. Those we love and care about the most will also pay a price as a result of our inability or unwillingness to get off high-center.

When we look at it objectively, it makes no sense at all to play tiddly-winks with our inertia. The benefits of the game are so incredibly short-lived! The reason we usually fail to take that next step is because we fear the price of our action. In reality, it costs far more to be stuck in a rut than it does to be light on our feet.

Interesting, is it not, that when the disciples went out two by two, they were told to leave behind their security blankets, house shoes, and iPods and basically go with what they had on their backs. Perhaps the reason behind those instructions is because inertia has a way of following our possessions the same way fleas thrive and multiply in sleeping bags.

Perhaps the most interesting thing about inertia is that, usually, we already know exactly where it has us by the throat. I can tell you at the drop of a hat what my next steps need to be, but that does not necessarily mean I am going to do anything about them.

In the C.S. Lewis classic, *The Screwtape Letters*, wasn't it the "affectionate Uncle Screwtape" who wrote something like this to Wormwood?

> *As your friend discusses with you the merits*
> *of turning over his life to God, don't argue him down and tell him*
> *he shouldn't do it. Instead, agree with him wholeheartedly*
> *that he should do it, but give him every excuse and reason why*
> *he should not do it today.*
> C. S. Lewis
> *The Screwtape Letters*

O God, help us to take the next step. Forgive us for clinging to our inertia as if it were a gift from you. Whatever it is, help us this very day, right now, to take the next step.

Personal Diagnostics no. 9

What are the characteristics of a relevant director?

When you look at the list of Core Characteristics and Added Qualities below, please do not become discouraged. None of us makes a perfect score on everything below, particularly on some days. However, considering these issues and taking mental notes on these Characteristics and Qualities will help us become better student choir directors in particular and stronger leaders in general. Don't be afraid to administer the test to yourself from time to time. The grades will not be posted!

Core Characteristics

- Strong love of God
- Commitment to serve the Lord in all circumstances
- Belief that God is love and speaks divine truth through scripture
- Compassion for students
- Organizational skills enough to get the job done
- Passion to teach teenagers to truly worship God
- Emotional connection with students
- Common sense enough to see that the future rests in teens
- Interest in the world of adolescence (and adolescents)
- Competent musician who finds joy in team participation and corporate success
- Musical technician growing in understanding of the choral idiom
- Joyful builder of teenage self-esteem
- Fun, winsome spirit
- A pleasant, unthreatening, non-anxious demeanor

- Knowledge that the youth choir experience makes a positive impact upon all, a significant impact upon some, and a profound difference for a few
- Willingness to give significant time and attention above the call of duty

Added Qualities

- Knowledgeable of the ever-developing teenage culture
- Willing to connect choir to ministry broader than just singing
- Active participant in the YouthCUE network
- Technologically savvy using creative youth choir application
- Literate in social networking
- Organizational skills to the level of building leaders
- Systematic and intentional building of strong relationships
- Commitment to build a real soundtrack for teenagers' lives
- Passion to make youth choir a truly life-changing experience for many
- Leadership gifts of mentoring and building lifelong friendships
- Willingness to spend nonmusical time for relationship-building
- Drive to produce incredibly meaningful events, lifetime memories
- Time (days, weeks, months) given to intensive prayer for individual kids and choir
- Private interviews or counseling sessions for kids before a major event
- Rites of passage for departing seniors

Personal Diagnostics no. 10

How can I teach my choir to sing with better dynamics?

1. *A director committed to training dynamics into his choir.* In order for a youth choir to sing with superb dynamic variation, contrast, shading, and nuance, the director must be absolutely committed to seeing (and hearing) it happen.

2. *Continual awareness among the students of their present dynamic levels.* Sensitizing a group of kids to the various volumes of singing is a time-consuming process, but once it is accomplished, the teenagers themselves will WANT to sing with various dynamic shadings. The director can begin by giving regular feedback about the level at which the kids are currently singing. "You just sang that phrase 'forte,' and that's what's called for. Good job, guys!" "That sounds a little strong to me, girls. Your phrase is marked 'mezzo piano,' but what I'm hearing is clearly 'mezzo forte.' Can you adjust that for us?"

3. *For beginning singers and even sometimes with veterans, creative, game-life exercises can sensitize kids to their dynamic levels.* Successful choir directors are essentially competent, creative teachers. Use your best teaching skills to engage, enrich, and enliven your rehearsals. Some of it will be planned, some will be spontaneous. The rule is that it must be interesting, productive, transferable to the music, and time-efficient (don't take too long getting your point across).

4. *Do not rely upon sound (decibel levels) only to provide the sensations of dynamics.* Train kids to feel within their mouths the difference between piano and forte, between pianissimo and fortissimo. Different dynamic levels produce various sensations in the mouth, head, and even within the lungs. In working choral dynamics, describe these sensations and allow the teenagers themselves to tell how each of the dynamic levels differs within them. There are no necessarily right or wrong sensations, but it will be very interesting to hear the descriptions from the teenagers. Everyone will become sensitized as those sensations are described in words.

5.   *Spend some time in every rehearsal discussing and producing choral sounds at various dynamic levels.* Sometimes, dynamics are easier to achieve with choral warm-ups and exercises than inside the phrases of music. This is particularly true of young or inexperienced choirs. Use vocalizing to set up the dynamic variations, and then the "lessons" can be plugged into phrases of music as needed.

Happy singing!

Personal Diagnostics no. 11

A lesson from Texas public schools

One day, I found myself in an environment where I have seldom recently been—inside a public school auditorium deep in the heart of Texas. I also found myself engaged in an activity which has become altogether too rare in my life and career.

I was an observer, pure and simple.

I had no responsibilities, no duties, and there were no expectations upon me. In fact, had I not carried a cell phone switched to "silent," no one in the world would have known where I was or how to contact me.

The event was a UIL (University of Texas Interscholastic League) choir contest. Choirs by the dozens, teenagers by the hundreds converged upon this large suburban high school to sing their concert contest repertoire and perform sight-reading exercises for adjudication.

Sitting and listening for perhaps three hours—who was counting?—I heard some stunning choral sounds. Of the numerous choirs performing, very few were truly substandard. Most performed their stuff in what I would consider to be good, excellent, or superb categories. A couple of choirs blew me away by their artistry, sensitivity, versatility, and stellar discipline.

I doubt I could have spent a more inspiring afternoon in any other chosen activity. These kids were wonderful! Many of the directors were marvelous. All seemed to be giving the event their very best effort ... and that in itself was a joy to hear and watch!

But before moving on, think about all the composers who dreamed up, wrote, edited, and signed publishing contracts on the music so the publishers could do final edits, go to the printer and distribute the paper bearing the proper musical notation.

It's a staggering thought to realize how much must come together in order for a great choir to function properly to provide education, instruction, and inspiration for a group of teenagers.

There's one other thing I'd like you to know about the UIL competition I observed. Please take note that clearly half of the music sung for competition was sacred music. Psalm texts, hymn settings, and artistic compositions featuring beautiful scriptural texts—these were staples of a choral festival in a very "secular" setting. Does this tell us anything?

I will be the first to admit that public school music and church music are different in many ways. For one thing, church musicians don't have grades to hold over students' heads. For another, school directors usually get to see their singers for about an hour per day five days a week. Church youth choir directors enjoy only about twenty percent of that time allowance.

However, for every disadvantage you can name that hampers church choirs, there is a corresponding advantage we have in providing actual ministry to students. There is no higher motivation for singing than the worship, ministry, and celebration of the Gospel, and no school can offer what any church can offer in this regard.

Watching the choir contest, I was struck by the amount of work it takes to begin, recruit, train, grow, and develop a choir comprised of teenagers. It is a huge task and one which knows no shortcuts. It's just plain old hard work, which has to be performed amidst the workaday, mundane, average days of adolescence.

One of the biggest temptations faced by youth choir directors is the lure of the quick fix. Often times pastors, church leaders and staff colleagues demand instant or quick success as a requirement for continuing the ministry of the student choir. This mindset subscribes to the philosophy which states or implies, "If it doesn't work quickly, then it's not worth pursuing. We can't wait two, three, or four years for this thing to take off."

We can't? Well, why not?

In some parts of the country, being surrounded by outstanding choral music is a natural thing for teenagers, a way of life they've always known. Those directors who serve in these places must understand that the church program, if it is to be attractive to teenagers, must be on an organizational par and in the same musical league as the best high school program in town. Bringing this into reality is much easier said than done.

Those of us who serve churches in regions where choral music seems a lost art have another set of challenges. It is up to us to set a musical standard that attracts, motivates and inspires kids, helping them to move ever close in their relationship to God as they grow musically. This, too, is much easier said than done.

The major keys are *choral competence, hard work,* and *a sufficient process of time.* This threefold approach, when coupled with the building of strong relationships with the kids and parents, is the closest thing to a formula we at YouthCUE can provide. There are no substitutes for consistent work, tenure, and relationship-building among students. But it is a job which needs desperately to be accomplished.

Personal Diagnostics no. 12

The how-to and benefits of a student choir repertoire system

Almost two decades ago, I put my youth choir on a "repertoire system" that has proved extremely helpful in my ongoing ministry with students. This is a concept I still develop today because it continues to be such an effective way to build a youth choir.

In my book, *Revealing Riches and Building Lives,* published in 2000, I suggested that our current anthem folder for youth choir contain ten to fifteen anthems of various styles and difficulty ranges. I further suggested that each rehearsal should touch on at least half those pieces in order to keep the rehearsal interesting and fresh. I and many other youth choir directors are big believers in keeping a good flow of music in front our students at all times. Otherwise, they will grow weary and bored with the same old songs. And yes, boredom can set in with an unconquered anthem as quickly as it can with one that has been polished and memorized. In fact, if a piece of music is too far over the singers' heads, they will become bored almost immediately, because they will feel unsuccessful trying to sing it. One of the key elements in building choral momentum is helping the group to feel successful on some level.

As an additional feature to all of the above, I always seek to maintain a repertoire system with my student choir. In other words, there needs to be a body of anthems, perhaps five or six, that they can successfully sing when the numbers are lower than normal, or when we're called upon to sing something at short notice.

In fact, I can provide a list of our current "repertoire list" which can be pulled forth, activated, and sung with ease and finesse with as little as one abbreviated rehearsal in preparation.

How does one achieve a repertoire along with learning bodies of new material?

It is accomplished over time, by hanging on to some of the group's most successful choral triumphs over several seasons. These anthems seldom represent the most difficult things my students have sung, because the most difficult anthems require fuller lofts and more singers to successfully perform. Each of the anthems in our repertoire is in the "easy to medium difficulty" category for my choir.

The amazing thing to me is how easy it is to keep these pieces warm. Once a choir has conquered an anthem, singing it once every four or five weeks will keep it in their heads and will even teach it to the new students who have no experience with it. For new students, if you can provide a recording of the anthem, it will help it take shape and keep its shape even more efficiently.

The repertoire list also must not be left to suffer long-term stagnation. In other words, replace one or two of the repertoire pieces each year with something new. It is also important to mention that repertoire selections should not necessarily be a "top ten" of the kids' favorites, although it's certainly possible to give them input into the decision. Generally the best repertoire anthems are those which are not faddish, will not be easily dated, and which can stand up to months and years of gentle rehearsing, perfecting, and polishing. Some youth choir music just won't stand up to that much rehearsal, and if light, trendy things become repertoire pieces, boredom is sure to set in.

What are the benefits?

First, you will never be without something to sing if you get into a bind when the preparation on a certain anthem just doesn't come together before your deadline.

Second, when called upon to sing for something at the last minute, you will have some good things from which to choose.

Third, if we select superb music with scripture texts for our repertoire, the positive power of scripture memory will be even more pronounced in the hearts of our students and congregations.

Personal Diagnostics no. 13

How do I keep students engaged for the whole rehearsal?

A series of books or educational videos could be produced to address this issue, but here are a few crucial insights.

Develop an understanding by everyone that time is limited, valuable, and not to be wasted. A challenging, though not overwhelming, "performance" schedule will be needed to instill a sense of urgency about getting down to business musically. If there's no deadline, there's little motivation for the kids to buckle down.

Discover a rehearsal pace which is so brisk that it leaves unfocused singers "in the dirt" from time to time. If you and your accompanist are on the same page— literally as well as figuratively—you can work together to constantly keep the rehearsal moving forward. Every now and then, the logistics of getting music up and ready needs to leave the kids "in the dust," momentarily behind, having to work hard to catch up with the director, accompanist, and sharpest kids who are right with you. Nobody likes being left behind!

Gently but firmly bring up the rear. Don't leave the kids in the dust for more than a couple of minutes. Once the dust has settled a bit, stop and give a brisk, 30-second "speech" about getting your music in order BEFORE the rehearsal begins and staying alert all the way through. Above all, stay good natured, on task, and positive, avoiding all temptations to put the kids down. It's important to keep your comments brief and motivational.

Pace the rehearsal so it is not so predictable. If we are able to capture students' interest, we will do it by being interesting. If our young singers begin to space out during the rehearsal, we probably need to take a hard look at our teaching methods and pacing. The rehearsal should not be so fast as to never take time to really fix problem areas, and yet, if we stop every time we hear a mistake, we will never sing more than three measures at a time. The pacing needs to involve variety, focus and relaxation, intensity and stress relief.

Engender passion and compassion. Be so passionate about your music and the project at hand that you naturally keep the rehearsal energized. At the same time, let your compassion for the kids show in everything you do!

Personal Diagnostics no. 14

How do I rally my students to commitment?

Ask teenagers why they are involved in youth choir, and you'll receive a variety of responses. But the answers you get will not just reflect the varied interest among different students; you will also receive a variety of responses from the same kid.

Few if any teenagers sing in youth choir for one simple, singular reason. The most successful programs throughout North America are those that meet a wide array of needs in the teenagers' lives.

Students often use language which reflects their budding understanding of what they are receiving in choir. They employ overused adjectives such as awesome, incredible, amazing, totally, way (as in "way cool"). Students will also cite being with friends, worshiping God, spreading the gospel, and helping others as the main reasons they stay involved.

Translated into the language of student choir leaders, here's what we know about why kids will consider being a part of our choirs and return year after year, rehearsal after rehearsal.

A fun journey towards a worthy goal. Any good teacher discovers the mystical balance of beginning the process where the kids *are* and quickly advancing them towards something higher, deeper, broader, richer, and more substantive. Take teenagers where they are and fail to advance at a good pace, and the unforgivable blight of boredom sets in. Shoot over their heads in the first few rehearsals and they're lost, discouraged, and defeated before they ever enjoy the ecstasy of a team victory. It is a crucial balancing act, and the director alone is ultimately responsible for finding it.

A consistent bridge to spiritual awareness. Even though school systems provide a good measure of structure, the primary goal of secondary education is the transmission of knowledge and practical understanding. The best teachers in our systems also creatively help their students discover how their required subject material relates to the building of strong character and spiritual stability. However, becoming spiritually mature is certainly not a prerequisite for graduation from any school—nor should it be. Student choir at its best ties together many loose ends in a teenager's learning process, providing students a hands-on, safe environment for learning, internalizing, practicing, and getting in touch with the spiritual dimension.

Stability amidst incessant change. For all their ADD-ness, adolescents crave stability and innovative routine. The world around them whirls with constant technological advancement, unending changes in social climates, friends moving in and out of their lives, adjustments large and small within the family, and churches facing the fear of irrelevance or extinction. It is no mystery why students long for something they can depend upon for stability and comfort. It is for this reason that we at YouthCUE have often said that the teenagers in our churches are by far the most traditional age group within our congregation. When we hit upon something that really works for students, a ministry or program or process which ignites their passions and inspires them to show up every week to be a part of it, they don't want anyone messing with it. Stability and true unity are such rare commodities in their worlds that once they experience them, they will hang onto them for all they are worth.

Simple beauty amidst pandemic noise. As driven as adolescents are to their iPods for "their music," there is still embedded in the soul of teenagers the deep longing to be a part of something truly beautiful. This desire is buried deeper in some kids than others, but we have discovered that it is a nearly universal phenomenon. The old "Sister Act" movies along with others such as "Mr. Holland's Opus" reminded us two decades ago that this is a timeless quality inside the hearts of youth.

Changing the world for the better. Most everyone wants to be an important part of something bigger than just ourselves. Whether the motivation is to help someone in need, to clean up the environment, to give a future to choral music, to feed someone who's hungry, to share the gospel, or all of the above, we all have an inborn desire to make the world a better place. Even the misguided desires of gang members are often based upon the desire to somehow right a wrong, stand up for a personal right, or to somehow improve a bad situation by a form of activism. In student choir, we have the opportunity to provide a productive avenue of activism that is totally positive and safe for every participant. The good accomplished has no downside.

Personal Diagnostics no. 15

Finding a good balance between rehearsal and "performance"

We place "performance" in quotation marks, because the vast majority of church youth choirs are involved in worship leadership, which is significantly different from a mere "performance." However, as choral directors, we readily understand the common pressure we all feel as we seek to prepare groups to produce at their top levels each time they sing. Here is some of what it takes to keep our kids in a good zone, developing a proper balance between preparation and up-front leadership.

A schedule of rehearsal and worship leadership that has been thoughtfully crafted, well-planned, and realistically developed. The responsibility for this task falls squarely upon the shoulders of the director. We must know our kids, their current level of musical ability, how motivated they are (and can become), and how they will likely respond to a challenge placed before them. It is with this data that we proceed to develop a schedule that will both encourage and affirm them.

A schedule of anthem "performance" which includes a fair range of difficulty and styles. Most choirs benefit from a repertoire which mixes easy anthems with moderately difficult pieces and tosses in a tough one every here and there. If the literature is consistently too simple, the group can become bored and unmotivated. On the other hand, it is just as easy to overwhelm the group by aiming too high on the difficulty scale. The chart below represents a good balance for most youth choirs:

Have a total of twelve (12) anthems before the group at all times.

- Three anthems: "Instant success" anthems which can be learned and memorized in one or two rehearsals.

- Four anthems: to be conquered, memorized, and polished over the process of three to four weeks.

- Three anthems: to be learned and performed within six to eight weeks.

- Two anthems: semester-long or even year-long projects that will demand the highest level of motivation, commitment, and discipline the group can demonstrate.

Remember to replenish your choir's folders, intentionally adding new selections to replace those already sung.

A choir schedule which is CLEARLY COMMUNICATED with all involved. The best-developed plans will fall woefully short if they are not properly and effectively communicated to the teenagers involved. This includes clear communication to the students' parents, as well. Remember to make your plans clear with your staff colleagues, particularly the minister to students. It is essential that all ministers responsible for teenagers be on the same page regarding scheduling and calendaring of events. Avoiding too many surprises will help all to feel more comfortable and confident.

Developing an effective rehearsal/singing schedule for your choir will not happen instantly. As we get to know our choirs and work toward greater balance, our effectiveness in scheduling will increase.